FEAST FOR THE SENSES

FEAST FOR THE SENSES

A Musical Odyssey in Umbria

LIN ARISON
and DIANA C. STOLL

Introduction by
MICHAEL TILSON THOMAS

Photographs by
NEIL FOLBERG

CHRONICLE BOOKS
SAN FRANCISCO

TUSCANY

⦿ Città di Castello

○ Montone

⦿ Gubbio

⦿ Umbertide

Castiglione del Lago

Isola Maggiore, Minore
Lake Trasimeno

○ Bosco

○ Magione

✪ PERUGIA

○ Solomeo

MARCHE

Pozzuolo Umbro

Isola Polvese

○ Castel del Piano

● Assisi

○ Spello

○ Torgiano

○ Deruta

○ Foligno

○ Città della Pieve

● Bevagna

○ Montegabbione (La Scarzuola)

● Montefalco

Castelluccio

UMBRIA

○ Campello sul Clitunno

Norcia

Monti
Sibillini

● Todi

Titignano ○

● Spoleto

○ Patrico

Orvieto ⦿

LAZIO

○ Terni

○ Narni

To the memory of Ted Arison,
to the Umbrians,
and to the spirit of music
that lives in the members of the
New World Symphony orchestra

INTRODUCTION

Michael Tilson Thomas

Lin Arison greets the world with curiosity and wonder. She sees the best in people and is always on the lookout for talent, taste, vision, quality of life, and spirit wherever and however they may appear. She is adventurous in her seeing, listening, traveling.

"I just want to look around the next corner," she'll say as she disappears, for hours or days, on a new quest. "Where's Linnie?" her husband, Ted, used to constantly query. Where is she? She's missing—and very much in action.

She is out there, somewhere off the beaten track, likely with no map or guidebook, forming her first impressions, keeping them fresh and very personal. Later, after she has got her own take on things, she'll consult with the folks she has met on her way, getting their take on what they consider the most essential experiences of their world, often surprising them with her appreciation of qualities she sees that they may have forgotten or taken for granted.

Lin builds friendships wherever she goes, and each new friend suggests to her an old one she feels would make a perfect match. So she begins to plan a way of bringing people together to share their talents, stories, and passions. The taste of an olive, a poem, a piece of music are essential things for Lin. She is also, of course, involved with many large projects that pass on that special knack of living a life in which the arts play a crucial role—these projects assure that young people, wherever they may come from, will have a chance to experience a life focused on the arts. "Make it possible for them to *taste* it," she'll say. "Let them taste it, and they'll begin to appreciate, understand, and—who knows?—make a place for art in their own lives and maybe even create their own art." What's important is that it all stays alive and vital.

Some of Lin's projects take place through the work of the New World Symphony and YoungArts (the core program of the National Foundation for Advancement in the Arts)—large, national organizations she founded with her husband, Ted. Over the last thirty years, the lives of thousands of young people have been enriched by amazing opportunities these organizations have made possible.

After Ted passed on in 1999, I think Lin went through a period of great soul-searching. Much of the impetus behind the New World Symphony and YoungArts had come from him, and she wondered how and in what way she would carry on. Lin found herself in writing books about the voyages of discovery she loves, and in sharing the experience with others. This book is a part of that process.

Lin had a wonderful idea: to open up her ongoing exploration of Umbria to members of the New World Symphony, to create the opportunity for them to share their music with people throughout this beautiful region. This idea was consistent with Lin's usual way of thinking and working: it would be a chance to bring old and new friends together—and it would be a voyage of discovery for everybody.

The project took place over two magical summers. There were concerts in Renzo Piano's fabulous new Santa Cecilia concert hall in Rome, and in palazzos, gardens, churches, country inns throughout Umbria—and on the spur of the moment anywhere along the road. It was spontaneous and great fun. Fast friendships were born on these trips. The spirit of the young artists, the beautiful music, and the land nurtured all they touched. It was excellent and it was personal.

Now, as the New World Symphony is approaching the opening of its new music meeting house, designed by Frank Gehry, it is a joy to look back to that experience of sharing, and forward to the project of making classical music's great tradition a more nurturing part of more people's lives.

Grapes, Poggio alle
Vigne, Torgiano

All photographs
2005–2006

ABOUT THIS BOOK

Lin Arison

It has been my good fortune to lead a life filled with voyages of many kinds. I have traveled to distant spots on the globe, where I have encountered new customs, traditions, people, and histories. And, like all of us, I have also experienced a life journey—a journey that has, at times, transported me to new places without even leaving my own living room. This book tells a story of both kinds of voyage.

I have shared tales of my travels in three volumes thus far. The first, *A Love Story in Mediterranean Israel*, is about moving to a new country—without speaking the language or feeling grounded there—and finding a way to create my own mode of communication with that wonderful land, which I now consider one of many beloved homeplaces. My second book, *Travels with Van Gogh and the Impressionists*, is about artists in whose work I found a comforting haven after the loss of my husband. In both projects, I experienced a kind of tandem learning process: I started out investigating one thing—Israel; turn-of-the-century French painting—and found myself discovering something unexpected: how a once-alien place can become a home; how art can serve as a powerful source of healing and resolution.

Through all my voyages, I have learned that being open to happenstance and new wonders is, for me, the optimum way to experience a journey.

Feast for the Senses began with the adventure of traveling in Umbria. During many of my explorations of the region, I was in the company of young musicians from the New World Symphony, as well as the orchestra's esteemed conductor and artistic director, Michael Tilson Thomas. Again, here was a double lesson. In the course of getting to know the beauties and the character of Umbria, I encountered something just as valuable: a new love and understanding of music. Though I was one of the founders of the New World Symphony in 1987, it took me many years to feel truly comfortable and welcome in the world of classical music. Today, I anticipate the opening of the orchestra's new Miami campus, designed by the brilliant Frank Gehry, with bated breath and a very full heart.

So in a sense, this book is about falling in love with two things at once—a process that was so exhilarating that I knew I had to share it.

I believe that my traveling companions, including all the musicians as well as my collaborators on this book—Neil Folberg, who made the magical photographs, and Diana Stoll, who helped put my story into words and contributed her own invaluable perspectives on Umbria—enjoyed seeing, listening, and tasting in Italy as much as I did. Each of them brought his or her own gifts to this endeavor. My greatest fortune is to have such friends join me and experience with them the joy of discovery.

In these pages, we invite you to accompany us on our voyage—and partake in this feast.

12   The musicians bowing, Villa Aureli, Castel del Piano

Evening concert, Villa Aureli, Castel del Piano

FEAST FOR THE SENSES

The pungent smell of goat breaks through my sleep to remind me where I am: in a clean, spartan bedroom on a farm at the top of the world in southern Umbria.

It is still pitch black outside, but this is September and morning is coming soon. I have a tendency to wake up very early so I can gather my thoughts. I close my eyes and think of what I have seen and tasted in the past days: what comes to mind first is the sharp yellow pecorino, sliced for me yesterday evening by Feliciano Bartoli, a member of the dynasty of farmers who owns this beautiful farm and *agriturismo* near Spoleto. The cheese, Feliciano's son Pietro told me, had been aged for five months; it was served with a dollop of honey that was two days old. The combined tastes were like earth and heaven.

The land here renders what is needed, and more. Like ancient music, it is timeless; it beckons without adornment. Yesterday evening I drove to the *agriturismo* along the mountain ridge of Patrico, followed by a full and contented moon. The family Bartoli is solicitous but pragmatic: they tend to their horses, their goats, their houses, their guests; they eat wonderfully (thanks to the talents of Marcella in the kitchen), and they sleep well at night. The lush beauty of this place is never lost on them, but they accept it as something they have known forever. The integrity of this existence is an inspiration.

In bed in this quiet room, even before I have my bearings, my thoughts turn to my late husband, Ted, and memories of the wonderful life we shared for more than three decades. He was a man who loved to live well and fully—and it was from him that I learned to appreciate many of the good things in this world. A brilliant and deeply creative man, Ted had a wonderfully successful career as the founder of the Carnival Cruise company. His success allowed us to found several organizations that foster the arts in the United States—notably the National Foundation for Advancement in the Arts (with its core program, YoungArts), in support of talented young people in all artistic disciplines; and the New World Symphony orchestral academy, under the adventurous artistic direction of its creator, Michael Tilson Thomas. These endeavors and Ted's business kept us both extremely busy; in many ways my love for him and my work with him defined my life for a long period of time.

Indeed, it is largely because of Ted that I am here in this bed on a mountain ridge in Umbria, waiting for the sun to rise.

After losing my husband in 1999, I was desperate to find something—anything—to take my mind to a new place, to bring some degree of warmth back into my life. I was fortunate to discover what I was looking for in the work and world of the Impressionist painters. I embarked on a five-year investigation into their lives and art, throwing my energies into the process with much enthusiasm. But as my research progressed and I saw that the project would eventually come to a closing point, I began to panic, feeling a void waiting for me at the end. I did not want to lose momentum, but what would follow? Where could I go next?

Italy was the answer. Of course. The joy I feel just at the mention of the place was enough to send me in this direction. My husband and I had had a long and intimate relationship with both the landscape and the people of Italy. Together over the years, Ted and I had launched several ships in Trieste and Venice, and I had traveled to the usual sites and places, from Rome to Portofino, Tuscany to Genoa. Those experiences gave me a taste of the grandeur of the country and the generosity and kindness of its people. Of my many travels with Ted, our trips to Italy provided some of my happiest memories.

And so, in 2003, in search of a viable subject for a new project, I invited my friend Gunilla Antonini to come with me for the first few days of an exploratory trip around Umbria and Tuscany. Gunilla's husband, Corrado, the head of the Fincantieri shipbuilding company, was a longtime friend and valued colleague of Ted's. Many a time Gunilla and I had trudged the shipyards together, discovering a welcome camaraderie that was soft and soothing against the backdrop of rivets, steel plates, dry docks, and massive ships. I looked forward to extending our friendship.

Gunilla was born in Finland but has lived in Rome for many years; she was greatly helpful in planning our trip. She started by offering a choice: we could stay at a small inn in a tiny village in Umbria or a large hotel in the region's capital city, Perugia. I didn't know Umbria well and was curious to find out what it was about from the ground up; I crossed my fingers and opted for small and charming.

A few weeks later, as our car pulled into the town of Torgiano, it was clear that this had been the right choice. Torgiano is a village made of stone: along its cobbled streets, three-story medieval palazzos look over a hillside of sunflowers. Over the front door of our hotel, Le Tre Vaselle, hang three majolica wine vessels—the *tre vaselle* of the establishment's name. The inn's exterior is fairly modest; like many structures in Umbria, its most important glories do not dole themselves out to first comers. Inside, Le Tre Vaselle is a surprising warren of lovely rooms, and its restaurant, Le Melograne, is celebrated throughout the region.

We checked in, but I was eager to explore the town, so rather than stay and unpack, I went out immediately to discover Torgiano. Along the Corso Vittorio Emanuele, one of the village's two main streets, beckoning like the entrance to Alice's Wonderland, was the glass door of the Museo del Vino. Just inside, I could see a beautiful carved stone spout, part of an ancient wine-press. My eye was held by it: the form was simple but exquisite, somehow even monumental—still, it was an unusual choice for a display.

Intrigued, I entered the building and wandered from room to room, amazed at the variety and quality of wine-related art and artifacts in this small, well-conceived museum. There were carafes from the third millennium B.C., colorful eighteenth-century ceramics, massive wooden and steel wine-presses, sacred and secular tomes on wine through the centuries: an entire history of viticulture. There were paintings of vineyards, a series of sculptures on the theme of "Wine and Myth," engravings by Annibale Carracci and Andrea Mantegna, a linocut of a bacchanal by Picasso, and a fascinating collection of book plates on the theme of wine. A large part of one room is devoted to a gathering of wafer irons, engraved metal forms on long arms, to be held over hot

The vineyards of Umbria are a vital component of the region's physical beauty: the hilly landscapes are everywhere divided into geometric forms with their neat, green striations. And the wines produced by those well-tended vineyards are integral to Umbria's character: the region's gastronomic pleasures would simply not be the same without them.

Long considered the rough stepsiblings of the "noble" Tuscan vintages, Umbrian wines have recently gained the reverence of œnologists around the world for their wonderful complexity and variety. The region's viticulture tradition may be traced back to ancient times: the Etruscans produced a sweet wine that was in demand throughout the Roman Empire. Today, vineyards thrive in the hospitable clay-and-sand-infused soil that covers much of region, welcoming both the warm sun and the gentle winds that keep the vines healthy.

The Lungarotti winery, based in Torgiano, produces vintages that are widely celebrated, including the iconic San Giorgio, Rubesco, and Rubesco Vigna Monticchio, and their signature white, Torre di Giano. The late Giorgio Lungarotti is credited with bringing Umbrian wines to worldwide attention with his earthy Sangiovese blends. And the Museo del Vino in Torgiano, conceived by his wife, Maria Grazia Lungarotti, provides a fascinating and comprehensive history of wine and wine making.

Orvieto is home to many of Umbria's great whites, made primarily from Grechetto and Trebbiano grapes (Antinori's Cervaro della Sala is a star from this neigborhood). The area around Montefalco is famous for its superb red wines, including the bold, powerful Sagrantino—perhaps the most prestigious wine of Umbria—made from the Sagrantino black grape varietal that is native to the region. Among the most celebrated producers of Sagrantino are Paolo Bea and Arnaldo Caprai, both in Montefalco. The so-called strada del Sagrantino (Sagrantino wine route) passes through the five Umbrian zones that yield this treasured beverage: Bevagna, Castel Ritaldi, Giano dell'Umbria, Gualdo Cattaneo, and Montefalco—a glorious itinerary indeed.

The Azienda Agraria Scacciadiavoli is one of the oldest wine-making estates in the Montefalco area. Like a sip of Sagrantino, the word "Scacciadiavoli" (SKAH-cha-dee-AH-vo-lee) rolls delightfully around on the tongue. Literally meaning "devil banisher," the name derives from an apocryphal tale, dating back to the seventeenth century, of a young woman said to have been possessed by a demon. The local exorcist prescribed red wine as the cure; the tonic worked, and the devil was driven off. The Scacciadiavoli cellars, built by commission of Prince Ugo Boncompagni in the mid-nineteenth century, are still in efficient working order today; otherwise, the winery is outfitted with state-of-the art technology. Indeed, Scacciadiavoli, now in the hands of the third generation of the local Pambuffetti family, runs like clockwork: the fermentation tanks are calibrated precisely, and beneath the stone archways of its immaculate, cool cellars, oak casks are carefully stacked, awaiting their moment of truth.

All this care pays off, of course, in the wine. Iacopo and Liu Pambuffetti, two of the younger members of this wine-making dynasty, are optimistic about the future of Scacciadiavoli, which has both posterity and ultramodern technology on its side. Sola Fides (faith alone) is the motto embossed on the coat of arms that hangs at the front entry to the cellars—though it would seem, along with faith, that hard work, devotion, and love are necessary to produce such astonishingly good wine.

In keeping with the characteristic Umbrian spirit, the vintners of the region are deeply proud of their products. Among aficionados, it has been said that Umbrian wines are "dignified, never submissive, but also straightforward and generous"—a description that could easily be applied to the people of Umbria as well.

embers to cook *cialde*, large, flat cakes that are traditionally spread with a sweet filling and enjoyed with *vin santo*. (Later on this trip, I acquired a tinful of *cialde*, which were treasured . . . and meted out slowly.)

I was very curious to know who was behind this wonderfully well-conceived collection. Gunilla informed me that it was her friend Maria Grazia Lungarotti and her late husband, Giorgio, who had created the wine museum, as well as the nearby Museo dell'Olivo e dell'Olio— another remarkable collection on the history of oil and olives. The couple also founded the great Lungarotti winery, which had virtually single-handedly raised the status of Umbrian wines—once considered somewhat inferior to lofty Tuscan vintages—to a world-class level. With her two daughters, Chiara and Teresa, Maria Grazia continues to expand her operation. Gunilla offered to introduce me to the family.

Maria Grazia's salt-and-pepper hair frames a face filled with grace and understanding. When we visited her majestic home in Perugia, I believe she recognized instantly that I had fallen passion-ately in love with Umbria: she gently took me under her wing. Chiara, her younger daughter, is an agronomist and takes charge of the Lungarotti vineyards, while Teresa plays an important role in running the family business. Teresa kindly invited me to her fiftieth-birthday "dance party." Somehow, I expected the gathering to include tradi-tional Umbrian folk dances and costumes—but of course there was nothing of the sort: it was more like a modern disco, with colored lights and masses of people bobbing and pulsating to the beat of loud music. The back lawn of Le Tre Vaselle was set up with a ban-quet of food and drink: a rowboat on the grass was filled with ice and freshly shucked oysters, moist lobsters in their red shells, and endless quantities of chilled Lungarotti Torgiano Spumante—which naturally ensured a very lively *festa*. It was one of my first experiences with a distinctly Umbrian characteristic: opening home and life readily to new friends. I would experience this welcoming spirit again and again over my time here.

Just outside Torgiano, set into hillsides of vineyards and olive groves, is Poggio alle Vigne, the Lungarottis' small *agriturismo*. The sense of absolute peace by these old stone buildings is palpable, and the views are breathtaking. When I visited Poggio alle Vigne and stood overlooking the nearby hills, somehow I knew I would return to Umbria later. A seed had been planted and was beginning to germinate.

For me, Umbria already held the reverential whisper of a secret and magical place. Its mountainous landscape is green and unspoiled, yet even during that first investigative trip, as I began to explore its villages, its life, its history, I found the region abounding with unheralded jewels. What a sweet discovery: this rare beauty, this contained calm in a world teeming with artificiality and hype. You have to slow your pace to match its primordial rhythms. As I learned to enjoy this new tempo, I became convinced that my next project should be a travel book about Umbria. My research had already begun, and in the most delightful way.

From Torgiano, it is a short drive northwest to Perugia, the medieval hilltop capital of Umbria.

The city's flat summit is cut through by the Corso Vannucci, a wide promenade stretching from the city's old fortress, the Rocca Paolina, on one end, to the *duomo* and the famous Fontana Maggiore on the other. The city exhibits a real magnificence, yet also the youthful energy of a university town. The streets are filled with chic students from all parts of the world, who attend the Università degli Studi di Perugia and the Università per Stranieri. In the summer the city is populated by music lovers who flock in to attend performances during the Umbria Jazz festival; superb concerts of all kinds also take place throughout the year in the city's many auditoriums. While Perugia may have ancient roots and a formidable history, the feeling in the streets is dynamic and very alive.

A logical place to start discovering Perugia is the great collection of Renaissance paintings and sculpture at the Galleria Nazionale dell'Umbria, located in the city's central Palazzo dei Priori. But I was interested in approaching Perugia—and, really, all of Umbria—in

a different way, with something more seminal, more earthbound. I wanted to meet some of the figures who make the region what it is and has always been: the artisans and craftspeople who continue in trades that have been practiced here for centuries. As it happened, the first three I encountered were women.

The Giuditta Brozzetti weaving studio is on Perugia's via Berardi, in a deconsecrated thirteenth-century church called San Francesco delle Donne. Marta Brozzetti, the great-granddaughter of the studio's founder, is a stylish young woman with short-cropped black hair and lively doe eyes. She collaborates with a team of weavers in this cavernous space, which retains a churchlike air and is vast enough to contain many looms. The textiles made here are authentic reproductions of medieval and Renaissance designs.

It is slow and painstaking work, and Marta often fears that she will be one of the last practitioners of this art. She showed me a table runner she was working on, a very complicated pattern with gold threads shooting through it; of such a piece, she told me, she can create a maximum of fifty centimeters a day. "After me," she says with a smile, "no one will be so insane." But rather than give up what she loves so deeply, she gives lessons in weaving, embroidery, and lace-making, in the hopes of enticing others to perpetuate her obsession.

A few streets away from the weaving atelier, on the via Fatebenefratelli, is the Studio Vetrate Artistiche Moretti-Caselli, the workplace of master glassmaker Anna Matilde Falsettini-Forenza. Like Marta, Anna derives from a long line of craftspeople, and the dynasty's youngest members are Anna's daughters Elisabetta and Maddalena. Their workplace is in an ornate Baglioni palazzo; the interior walls are still graced with intricate painted patterns, and the light inside is diffused by leaded-glass windows. This is clearly a working studio of long standing. One area, the so-called *stanza dei colori*, or "color room," is lined with shelves of vials filled with powders of every hue, originally used to tint glass. Anna and her team produce stained-glass windows for churches and cathedrals and provide lessons to the next generation of craftspeople.

Studio Vetrate Artistiche Moretti-Caselli, Perugia. **Opposite**: George Curran and Elisabetta

Forenza. **Above**: Myroslava Ivanchenko

CELEBRATED VISITORS TO UMBRIA

Umbria has hosted scores of well-known visitors over the centuries, from the marauding Hannibal, who in 217 B.C. famously defeated the Roman army near Lake Trasimeno, to the young musicians of the New World Symphony orchestra, who made more peaceful conquests here in the early twenty-first century. In the interim, many other celebrated travelers have made their way to the region.

Umbria's wondrous landscape has of course been the subject of much praise. In 1581 French writer Michel de Montaigne admired "the sight of a thousand varied hills . . . the landscape [is] of a beauty and richness beyond the power of a painter to imitate." Danish fabulist Hans Christian Andersen was enchanted by Castiglione del Lago: "We passed Castiglione, going through a luxuriously beautiful country, with olive woods and vines. . . . Near Lake [Trasimeno], where Hannibal fought, I saw on the road-side the first native laurel tree. . . . We enjoyed the most beautiful sunset; such a gorgeousness of colors I never shall forget."

Perugia, Umbria's capital city, has been noted by such writers as Henry James, who stated that the visitor's "first care must be not to be in a hurry—to walk everywhere, very slowly and very much at random, and gaze good-naturedly at anything his eye may happen to encounter," as well as by Charles Dickens ("Perugia, strongly fortified by art and nature, on a lofty eminence, rising abruptly from the plain, is glowing, on its market day, with radiant colours"), George Sand ("Perugia is university city, a poetical place—one of the old Italian centres of beauty and learning"), Nathaniel Hawthorne ("the strange, precipitate passages which, in Perugia, are called streets"), and Virginia Woolf ("I have never seen such a lovely city").

In 1831 composer Felix Mendelssohn suffered through an unfortunate carriage ride from Rome into Umbria: the coachman was surly and abusive, the carriage's axle broke en route, and, to make matters worse, he was accompanied by "three Jesuits . . . and a most disagreeable Venetian woman. . . . a wretched state to be in!" The trip was at least partly redeemed by the region's offerings: "If nature had not bestowed on us the bright moonshine at Lake [Trasimeno], and if the scenery had not been so wonderfully fine, and if in every town we had not seen a superb church, if we had not passed through a large city each day as we journeyed on, and if—but you see that I am not easily satisfied." Richard Wagner sojourned at Perugia's Hotel Brufani in 1880, and it is said that the basis of his opera *Tannhäuser* derives from the legends of Umbria's Sibilline mountains.

In his *Italian Journey*, Johann Wolfgang Goethe describes visits to Umbria; in his passage about the Ponte delle Torri—words that are today etched in stone by that Spoleto monument to be read by visitors—he notes "the ten arches of brickwork [which] have stood there so calmly over the centuries." Goethe saw a "noble spirit" in three of the city's ancient structures—the bridge, the amphitheater, and the *duomo*: "A second Nature, one that serves civic goals, that is what their architecture is."

Poet and novelist Hermann Hesse was profoundly moved during his own youthful perambulations on foot around Umbria in 1901. In his novel *Peter Camenzind* is this passage:

I had the noblest and most delicious experience of my youth: wandering through the rich green Umbrian hills. . . . I picked lemons and ate them on hills glistening with sunlight, spent my nights in little villages, sang and composed poems within myself. . . . Each day new sources welled up within me and I gazed onto the clear and festive landscape as into the benign eyes of God.

Umbria continues to inspire, as it has for centuries, with that same clear and festive landscape, scarcely changed since the ancient days.

The third artisan I encountered was Mariaelisa Leboroni, whose woodblock prints can be found all around Umbria. I came across her work at a shop in Torgiano, where I was drawn to a small, thick notebook with a cover illustration of a smiling fat frog: it was in this notebook that I first began recording my impressions of Umbria. I visited the artist at her studio near Perugia not long after. There I watched as Mariaelisa carefully whittled designs into blocks of wood—as artists have done for centuries—and then fitted this wooden treasure into a very modern metal press. Out the other end came papers printed with Mariaelisa's fanciful designs: olive trees with ladders propped against them, and nets drawn across the green grass to catch the olives at harvest-time; a field of yellow sunflowers with the town in the distance; and my beloved laughing frog.

Mariaelisa's work, like that of Anna Falsettini-Forenza and Marta Brozzetti, revealed something important to me about the character of Umbria. It is a place of extraordinary pragmatism: its artists and artisans work hard and maintain traditions without pretension or arrogance.

Although they have the good luck to live in a region of almost inexpressible beauty, they do not flaunt it as they might. I found these attributes to be intensely refreshing.

Gunilla went back home to Rome, so I finished off that brief tour of Umbria on my own, and then moved on to Tuscany, which seemed strangely dull to me now. I had of course visited Siena and Florence in the past and been enthralled by their wonders. It seemed unimaginable that such storied places could hold little interest, but on this visit they struck me as overblown and unappealingly *sophisticated*. Nothing was as alive, as real, as Umbria for me. I was ready for more.

My next trip to Italy, however, was made for other reasons. In 2004 the New World Symphony was to perform two concerts at Rome's Santa Cecilia hall, with Michael Tilson Thomas conducting—and I would be traveling to Italy with them.

Michael—who is referred to as "MTT" by both friends and strangers—is of course one of the great musicians of our time. He has also been a good friend and, in a sense, a mentor to me in the world of music. Although he is a gentle and charming man, he can have an intense presence—and I'll confess that I was somewhat intimidated by him when Ted and I first met him more than twenty years ago. Indeed, I was intimidated by the whole vast, then-unfamiliar world of classical music.

MTT founded the New World Symphony with Ted and me in 1987 as a training ground for gifted young musicians. In the years since, the NWS has blossomed, and under MTT's guidance it has earned a reputation as one of the world's premiere musical programs for young people. As an orchestral academy, the NWS brings in post-conservatory musicians—most of them in their early and mid-twenties—for three intensive years of training and performance, at the end of which they leave with the best possible credentials to apply for permanent positions in other top-grade orchestras.

The story of the NWS's founding bears retelling. In the early 1980s, our friend Grant Beglarian (then president of the National Foundation for Advancement in the Arts) suggested to Ted and me that the foundation should begin an academy for young musicians. Ted—who had a very good ear and imagined a disorderly group of scratchy violins, off-key French horns, and squawking tubas—at first didn't cotton to the idea in the least.

A couple of years went by, and Ted and I paid a visit to our friends Georg and Valerie Solti in London. We were there for only one night, and Valerie had told us that Georg had a concert that evening in Croydon, just outside London; he would be conducting the European

Community Youth Orchestra (now known as the European Union Youth Orchestra). She suggested that we attend the concert and then all have dinner afterward, and Ted and I happily agreed. In Croydon, we sat down to hear what these young musicians could do. I don't know if Ted was at all skeptical before they began playing, but within three notes, he turned and whispered to me that he was ready to rush home to Miami to start a training orchestra. He was thrilled by the talent, verve, and freshness with which the young musicians played every note.

Back in the United States, Ted immediately contacted Grant Beglarian and asked if he had suggestions as to who would be the right person to run this new orchestra. Without hesitation, Grant named Michael Tilson Thomas; he explained that for some time MTT had wanted to create an orchestral academy. The young conductor had just the right energy and drive—and all the experience, discernment, and talent—needed to pull this off.

Not long after, in late 1986, Ted and MTT sat down together for a meeting at the St. Regis Hotel in New York. MTT had clearly thought through all the elements that would be needed for this enterprise, and he made the financial and organizational realities very clear to Ted. He also seemed convinced that, once Ted understood those needs, the project would be abandoned. MTT began to list all the requirements—staff salaries, rehearsal and performance spaces, dormitories, stipends—and Ted nodded. MTT continued down the list: travel expenses, honoraria for visiting artists, marketing, publicity, a music library . . . and, to his amazement, Ted continued to nod in agreement. The deal was struck: the training orchestra would be named the New World Symphony—an allusion to Miami, a burgeoning "new world," gateway between the Americas. As the meeting wrapped up, Ted had just one final question: How long would it take to create such an orchestra? MTT thought for a moment and then answered: "Two years, at least—more likely two and a half."

Ted smiled. "Let's do it in six months," he said.

The New World Symphony orchestra's first concert took place at Miami's Gusman Center for the Performing Arts on February 4, 1988.

As for me, when Ted and MTT were first discussing the idea of this "orchestral academy," I was already feeling distinctly out of my realm. Although I had studied the piano briefly as a kid, I knew next to nothing about classical music. Ted, on the other hand, had shown great talent as a musician in his youth, and he had an incisive understanding of music and knowledge of the classical repertoire. I had the sense that classical music existed in a separate, elite world that I would never be part of and never comprehend. In a moment of candor, after I'd come to know MTT a bit better, I remember saying to him that I was afraid I was going to embarrass myself and him with my lack of knowledge. "How can I help create this orchestra," I asked him, "when I don't know anything about music?"

MTT looked at me a little quizzically. "You're alive," he said simply. "Being alive gives you all you need to know. Just *love* it."

What a relief! Just love it—I thought I could manage that. Once this idea was planted in my head, I found that watching our young orchestra members rehearse was absolutely captivating, and soon I began to feel at home in concert halls as well. MTT's words have continued to echo inside me over the years. And that cardinal rule, to allow oneself simply to *love* great things—music, art, people, places—without permitting fear of the unknown to obstruct the enjoyment, has opened me up to countless invaluable experiences . . . not least among them my time in Umbria. This openness has in turn led me to learn a great deal—sometimes unwittingly—so that now my knowledge of classical music is far more solid than it was (though I will never be an expert!).

In Rome, I was very happy to sit in the audience at the Santa Cecilia concert, as our ninety young musicians played Gustav Mahler's Symphony no. 5 with such gusto and nuance. The auditorium was packed, and MTT—an acknowledged master of Mahler—elicited a performance from the orchestra that brought the very discriminating international audience to its feet in a tumultuous ovation.

After that concert I met several people to whom I would soon become close: MTT's friend Corinne Laurie introduced me to Sarah di Belmonte, who has a home in Spoleto, and to Piero and Andrée Colonna

Above: Musicians arriving in Rome. **Opposite:** Michael Tilson Thomas

di Paliano, who live just outside Orvieto. That night, I also met Lithian Ricci, a lively young woman and a wonderful painter who is based in Milan and Tuscany. Although I did not know it yet, all these friends would provide crucial help in my explorations and plans in Umbria.

The Rome concerts were a great success and received rave reviews. MTT was well satisfied with the performances, and now had a few days without concrete plans before he had to return to the United States. Fatefully, he asked if I had any suggestions of where he might spend them. I offered to show him some of the Umbrian sights I had so enjoyed discovering.

The following day, MTT and his partner, Joshua Robison, and I headed to Todi for lunch. Like many Umbrian towns, Todi is picturesquely situated at the top of a green hill. Although the Ristorante Umbria has an open stone terrace overlooking the wide plain below, this was February and it was chilly, so we chose a table inside, close to the wood fire on which roasted the meats—*palombaccio* (squab), lamb—offered on the day's menu. We had noticed a tantalizing display of olives, cheeses, and homemade *salumi* as we entered the establishment, and we decided to share a platter of antipasti. With the meal, we had a bottle of Sassicaia; it was my first experience with this splendid wine from the Maremma, and it was very memorable. Its dark warmth and subtlety perfectly matched this place and these friends.

Indeed, the entire afternoon is one I will always remember. MTT marveled at the olives, at the fact that each one tasted and looked different from the rest—raised, as they were, naturally, in the Italian way, not artificially cultivated into fat, uniform globes. Every flavor we sampled that day stood strongly on its own. Every part of the repast was lovingly prepared, from ingredients lovingly grown. At the end of the meal, MTT said that while he has had many entrancing musical experiences, this had been a very powerful life experience for him.

I was touched by his response. Food can create such epiphanies, and while Italy seems to teach that lesson every day, I believe it is something many Americans still have to learn. I thought of my son Michael, back home in the United States. He owns and runs an organic farm in

36   *Lemons*, Villa Aureli, Castel del Piano

North Carolina, where he has recently sponsored a program to teach youngsters how to grow, cook, and learn from food. I'd talked to Michael recently on the phone, and he told me he was standing in his fields; as we spoke he picked a stalk of broccoli straight from the earth and took a bite. His very real joy in the vegetable's tenderness and goodness was as deep and meaningful as MTT's wonderment at tasting these olives. I felt a rush of pride that my son is working to bring this comprehension of the beauty of food to the next generation, as well as intense happiness to find myself in a country that embodies that understanding.

After leaving the Ristorante Umbria, MTT, Joshua, and I walked the *scalette* of Todi: the stone stairways that weave between the buildings and lead down the mountainside, punctuating the stone townscape with slivers of the surrounding golden lands and sky.

Recalling the success of the recent concerts, I asked MTT how he had come to focus on Mahler. He told me that he well remembered his first moment of connection to the composer. When he was around fourteen, he went to a schoolmate's house in Los Angeles. As his friend was not yet back from school, Michael waited for him in the home's library. There, sitting on a sofa, he listened intently to the record that was playing. MTT was already an accomplished musician, but this was unlike anything he had considered before. He was dumbfounded. He recalls today that all the emotions in the music seemed fully and profoundly familiar to him; he recognized them immediately. It was Mahler. That familiarity is still clear to audiences today when MTT conducts Mahler— and his familiarity becomes ours.

From Todi, MTT, Joshua, and I drove northeast through a green and umber valley to the nearby ancient town of Bevagna. One of the few villages in Umbria that is built on low ground, Bevagna is—even without distant vistas—truly magical, graced with both Roman artifacts and medieval edifices. Each year, the town hosts the festive Mercato delle Gaite, during which its inhabitants don clothes, cook meals, and produce crafts in the manner of the Middle Ages—each neighborhood (or *gaita*) competing furiously against the others. Today, however, Bevagna's narrow alleyways were quiet: it was the afternoon siesta time. Speaking

OLIVE OIL

If Umbria is Italy's "green heart" (as the guidebooks always have it), then olive oil is the green lifeblood that keeps it pumping. One might venture to say that there does not exist an Umbrian kitchen without a vial, a bottle, a can, or a jug of the precious liquid ready for daily use.

Olive oil has been cultivated in this region at least since Etruscan times. The olive tree—with its distinctive gnarled grace and small, silvery leaves—is a long-lived specimen; some of the groves that dot the landscape today were planted hundreds of years ago. Around the region, it is said that good olive oil is a product of *la madre umbria* (Mother Umbria), and many towns—including Spello, Trevi, and Gualdo Cattaneo—host regular celebrations of the nectar. The soil here is conducive to growth, the drainage is ideal, the sun is strong but rarely punishing: it is no wonder the ancient trees are still happily producing their miraculous fruit year after year. For many Umbrian families, the yearly *raccolta* (harvest) is a much-anticipated gathering of friends, who, armed with ladders and baskets, work together to pick, sort, and deliver the year's olives to the local press. In return for this cooperative effort, each family is then rewarded with a portion of the rendered oil.

Francesco Gradassi is extremely serious about his olive oil. He is the director of the Azienda Agraria Marfuga, near Campello sul Clitunno, producers of some of the region's finest olive oil and winners of many national awards. Representing the fourth generation of oil makers (his family has been in the business for more than two hundred years), Gradassi has the palate of a great connoisseur, and he can tell you anything you'd like to know about the history of olive cultivation in Italy. A visit to the Marfuga *fabbrica* includes a tour of their impeccable facility and a tasting of a variety of extra-virgin olive oils, from the fruity *novello* to the dark, delicious, and very intense *affiorante*—each drop worth a thousand words.

Olive oil is essential to Umbrian cuisine. Even many sweets—including the delicious *cialde* wafers—are enhanced, and their flavors made more complex, by the addition of *un bicchiere* (a glass) of olive oil. One of the simplest and most exquisite of Umbrian *bruschette* consists of only two ingredients: toasted bread drizzled with the best and most aromatic olive oil available—likely produced just down the road. (The more extravagant gourmand may wish to sprinkle on a little salt.)

A very typical Umbrian *primo* is the beautiful *zuppa di farro*, a smooth, pale soup made with a popular local grain. (Often mistranslated as "spelt," *farro* is in fact a far friendlier and faster-cooking ingredient, which is becoming increasingly available in the United States.) This is one of many local dishes that is simply not the same without the indispensable addition of olive oil just before serving.

Zuppa di Farro
Serves 4

Ingredients

2 tablespoons extra-virgin olive oil
1 large onion, sliced
2 celery stalks, chopped
2 carrots, peeled and chopped
1 tablespoon minced garlic
1 cup *farro* (if unavailable, substitute spelt)
1 cup dried cannelini beans, soaked for several hours or overnight
2 cups chopped tomatoes (canned are fine)
6 cups good stock
1/4 cup chopped fresh parsley
Salt and pepper to taste
Freshly grated Parmesan or aged pecorino cheese
Olive oil for drizzling

In a large, heavy pot, heat the oil and sauté the onion, celery, and carrots until soft (about 10 minutes). Add the garlic and stir until aromatic. Add *farro*, beans, tomatoes, and stock.

Bring to a boil, and then lower heat to simmer. Cook until *farro* and beans are tender, about 2 hours, adding more stock (or water) as necessary if mixture becomes too thick. Stir in parsley, salt and pepper, then cook another 5 minutes. When all ingredients are tender, the soup may be puréed (if desired) in a food processor or with a wand-blender. Taste and adjust seasoning.

Serve with grated cheese and a drizzle of excellent-quality olive oil in each bowl.

little, we wandered to the main square, the Piazza Filippo Silvestri, and from there into the Teatro Francesco Torti, the lovely little auditorium located in the Palazzo dei Consoli.

Inside, the theater is a red and gold jewel box, with a frescoed ceiling and a marvelous stage backcloth showing the meandering Clitunno River, painted during the theater's recent renovation by the local artist Luigi Frappi. Joshua and I positioned ourselves in the theater seats, and MTT could not resist walking onto the stage, where he clapped his hands to test the theater's acoustics.

With that clap, in that charming Umbrian theater, an idea came to me, a marvelous and really irresistible fantasy. What would happen if two wonderful elements were brought together: the music of the New World Symphony and the landscapes of Umbria? What did they have in common? Well, to me both are thrilling, timeless, and filled with vitality. I had found myself falling in love with both without quite realizing it; I had wandered into both without knowing exactly where I was, only to be smitten completely. Those seemed like very important parallels to me.

I began to visualize the young NWS musicians playing together outdoors, against the backdrop of these breathtaking hills. I imagined listening to strains of music under the open Italian sky.

The Teatro Torti is a very beautiful theater, but my thoughts as I sat there that day were of concerts performed in the open air—unconstrained, unconfined, no tickets to buy, no seats to reserve—these musical, cultural, and atmospheric wonders coming together in what would surely be a feast for the senses. As they had so many times before, MTT's words came to mind: "Just *love* it." I had learned to love it, and I wanted to share that experience with others.

There can be no action without the notion that precedes it. As the seed of this idea took root, I talked with MTT. He gave me one

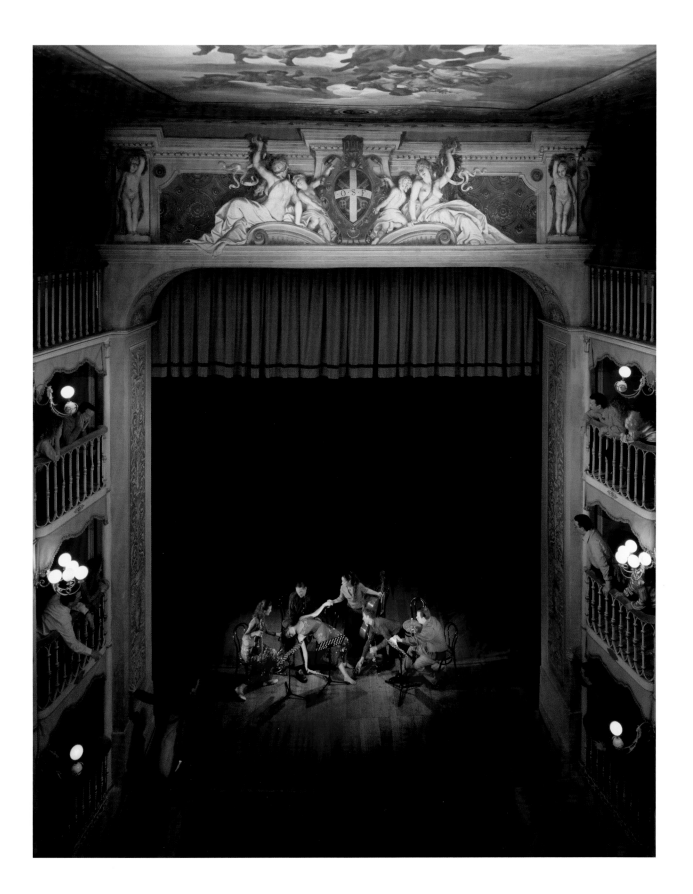

FESTE AND SAGRE

Tulips, saints, truffles, crossbows, pigeons, Dante, jazz, kite flying. And let's not forget snails. What do these things have in common? They are among the themes celebrated at Umbria's yearly *feste* and *sagre*—town festivals focused on a specific subject, generally involving much food and drink, traditional costumes and customs, and sometimes very competitive games.

Bevagna's Mercato delle Gaite is a wonderfully colorful weeklong celebration, and a typical *festa* in that the town is divided into rival factions that compete—ostensibly in good spirits, but actually quite fiercely—over everything from the most authentic demonstration of medieval arms to the most succulent oca *arrosto* (roast goose). The contentiousness in Bevagna can become so heated during the festival that residents of one neighborhood may refuse to speak to those of another—even family members may turn against one another for the week.

One of Italy's oldest annual festivals is Gubbio's Festa dei Ceri, which has taken place every May 15 since at least the twelfth century (and some believe it dates back to pagan times). For this gathering, the city's affiliations are divided into three parts, each represented by a group of strong young men willing to don traditional clothes and run at top speed through the town and finally up the very steep Monte Ingino to the Basilica of Sant'Ubaldo, bearing a massive wooden platform and effigy of a saint: a burden of more than six hundred pounds per team. (Historically, the effigies were made of wax, or *cero*, hence the festival's name.) The Festa dei Ceri attracts masses of spectators from all over the region to Gubbio. Nearly a millennium into its existence, the festival still has an air of delirium and mysticism.

There seems to be no town in Umbria too tiny to boast a regular *festa*. Castiglione del Lago celebrates kites every other spring with Coloriamo i Cieli; Foligno (where the first printed edition of Dante's *Divina Commedia* was produced in 1472) hosts the Celebrazioni Dantesche each April; and the handful of residents in the village of Pozzuolo Umbro pull out all stops in August in honor of the *ciacciola* (traditional Umbrian flat bread). On a larger scale, there are of course Spoleto's Festival dei Due Mondi and Perugia's popular Umbria Jazz festival.

More modest—though certainly no less momentous—is the annual Sagra della Lumaca, the snail festival, in the tiny town of Cantalupo di Bevagna, held each August. The menu of the celebratory feast is distributed well in advance:

Antipasto di lumache
(snail antipasto)
Bruschetta all salsa di lumache
(bruschetta with snail sauce)
Tagliatelle all salsa di lumache
(tagliatelle with snail sauce)
Polenta all salsa di lumache
(polenta with snail sauce)
Lumache alla contadina
(snails country style)
Lumache arrosto
(roast snails)
Lumache al sugo
(snails with sauce)

Buon appetito!

of his enigmatic looks at first, but I believe that Umbria had spoken to him as well. He agreed that this fantasy just might work.

So my Umbria project became something much more complex and exciting than I had originally envisioned. It became an endeavor of many months' planning and years in production—time well spent and joyfully given.

The concept took shape early on: we would bring a selection of musicians from the NWS—enough for a chamber-music ensemble—to Italy for a series of recitals and concerts. My mission was to scope Umbria to find just the right locations for the young musicians to experience.

I have collaborated on several projects over the years with the photographer Neil Folberg, and I knew that I needed his talents here as well. I would ask Neil to apply his abundant creative energies to photographing the young people in situ. I hoped thus to gather the ingredients for a publication that would be unabashedly seductive—and that might lure even those who were intimidated, as I had once been, by this misunderstood world of classical music. The resulting book is what you hold in your hands. Little did I know how much fun the process would be, or how successful.

The Message
(**left:** Alucia Scalzo and Rick
Basehore; **right:** Emilia Mettenbrink
and Julie Smith), Spoleto

It would take more than a year to organize two series of concerts—one in 2005, and the second in 2006—and the musicians' trips to Umbria.

I followed up on several contacts that I had met through MTT after the 2004 Rome concerts, and cast out a net for possible venues for performances and photo shoots. I found that the Umbrians were incredibly kind: they were ready to open their doors, introduce me to new friends, and point out fantastic sites in the region that were little known and rarely visited, even by most Italians. Piero and Andrée Colonna offered the grounds of their home overlooking Orvieto as a setting for one of Neil's tableaux, and Lithian Ricci suggested her own family's estate in Tuscany's Maremma as a possible concert site. Teresa Severini introduced me to her friends Sperello and Carla di Serego Alighieri, who have a wonderful palazzo in Castel del Piano, near Perugia. Again and again I found myself being adopted by residents of Umbria who were deeply proud of their region's beauties and heritage and eager to share them. In addition to this warm welcome, I was treated to gracious thanks for the project we were so enthusiastically bringing to their region.

I greatly enjoyed those months of planning, as they gave me a chance to really get to know the nooks and crannies of Umbria, even as I was making new friends. And Neil needed at least this much time to conceptualize his photographs: he visited sites with me, immersed himself in Italian art and culture, and formulated ideas for costumes, settings, and themes. Adam Zeichner, the director of operations and personnel of the New World Symphony, saw to it that every aspect of the planning went smoothly, and he helped Neil pick out a group of NWS musicians who would make up a solid chamber orchestra. Adam traveled with us during both series of concerts, and his presence was invaluable: he arranged flights; set up rehearsals, photo shoots, and concerts; worked with the terrific GBang production team from Spoleto; and generally coordinated myriad details while shepherding his flocks. (His voluminous lists have been vital to the reconstruction of this story.)

Finally, the concert venues were all arranged; the hotel rooms were reserved for the musicians and the crew; the minivans were ready for transportation; the photo-shoot sites had all been selected; and the caterers, costumers, makeup artists, and even a few animal wranglers had been appointed. Invitations to the concerts had been sent out to a network of people—Europeans, Americans, other friends, and friends of friends. We were as ready as we would ever be.

The first group of musicians arrived at the Relais San Clemente in Bosco, near Perugia, in the spring of 2005. I heard the tires crunching on the gravel as the bus pulled up to the beautiful Benedictine-monastery-turned-hotel, and I then watched nine very hungry young people pour into the hotel's dining room. Lunch, as always, began with pasta, and as the musicians sat and chatted, their eyes widened in delight as they ate. Clarinetist Robert Woolfrey, who had never visited Italy before, declared this simple dish of noodles the best food he had ever eaten; little did he know that it would be followed by course after course, each more delectable than the one before.

Somehow, in the bustle of exploring, programming, and making arrangements, I had not taken into account the fact that this trip would have a life-affecting impact on these young performers. Watching them eat lunch that day, I realized that this would be an unexpected and wonderful component of this adventure—and what a perfect exchange: these musicians, who were bringing so much to Umbria, would benefit unforgettably from the experience as well. Rob, who now plays second clarinet with the Cleveland Orchestra, recently confided in a letter to me that his Italian journey had a vital impact on his performance. "I am letting the music speak for itself—much like the food of Umbria speaks for itself!" he wrote, further explaining that when music, like food, is of the highest quality, it needs very little embellishment or "seasoning."

Trombonist George Curran has said that what he experienced in Italy "confirmed a life's goal: to balance purpose with a quality of living that allows you to enjoy life." Umbria, he feels, is a place where "these

goals are being lived out by so many people; they figured it out long ago." Violinist Marc Rovetti was profoundly inspired by the timeless buildings and treasures of Umbria: "Being in towns that are hundreds of years old put my whole life in perspective. I somehow understood my place in human history, and it brought me a lot of comfort.... People have been searching for centuries for the meaning of it all, and to have the cathedrals and great art all around you, putting this quest into tangible form, is awesome. History seems so much more relevant when you are standing in the middle of it."

As musicians, the NWS members were somewhat perplexed at the documentary and photographic aspect of the project. We had a film crew with us for much of the 2005 trip, and of course Neil's photographs were a central part of the project. These youngsters are used to hard work and performing, but *music* is their raison d'être—not posing for photographs. This presented occasional challenges as the weeks and months went on, but I think the photographs testify both to Neil's talents and to the musicians' ultimate mastery of the process.

Neil and I had chosen San Clemente as the first location for a shoot because of the great expanse of green grass immediately behind the hotel and the vista of blue hills in the distance: a perfect backdrop for the image that Neil had in mind. The following morning, we set things up. While pianist Ciro Fodere waited outside at a keyboard, Neil and his assistant, Max Richardson, positioned a battery of lights to ensure photographic crispness. When the switch was turned on for the lights, however, there was a sharp explosion and the generator threw off enormous sparks. Everyone dove for cover—Ciro hurled himself under the piano for maximum protection. An auspicious beginning: fireworks!

Fixing the generator took a while, and the musicians took advantage of the break to go practice. As aspiring young professionals, the NWS musicians are astonishingly disciplined. Until this trip, I really did not know that they practice at least six hours a day, and often more if they are preparing for performances. Indeed, we had to work the photo sessions around those practice hours—which was not a problem, since Neil favored shooting early in the morning or late in the afternoon

rather than during the stark, shadowless midday. Thus the warmest hours of the day were filled with tangled passages of music coming from every room as the young people practiced for the upcoming concerts. I sat in on many rehearsals and found myself deeply touched by the musicians' fierce concentration and determination to make the music as full of meaning as it could be. Violinist Jennifer Best admitted to me that sometimes her focus is so intense when she is practicing that she can forget the impact the music may have on listeners. She was surprised to see tears in my eyes during one of the group's rehearsals.

Our first concert took place at the home of Lithian Ricci's family, the Castello di Segalari at Castagneto Carducci in the Maremma, northwest of Umbria.

The musicians were positioned on the lawn of this magnificent estate, under a wing of canvas strung from tree to tree. The audience was a very distinguished group—many of them friends of the Riccis'—who sat in a circle of chairs and listened enthralled to Mendelssohn, Debussy, Ravel, and Vivaldi while gazing out over the Tyrrhenian Sea. Even MTT— who is familiar with the challenges posed by performing outdoors—was very pleased with the event and its reception.

The next day we took off in minibuses to get ready for the first performance in Umbria proper. It would take place at the Castello dell'Oscano, near Perugia: a mighty, gray stone castle—complete with turrets—hidden from view among the thick surrounding forests. Oscano's two main towers and a connecting parapet wall were built in the late 1300s for the use of papal soldiers in the ongoing battles against Tuscany. Four hundred years later, the rest of the castle was constructed, with the old walls incorporated. The *castello* has a history of being used as a place for artists to come and entertain its inhabitants. I

Previous pages, left: *The Little Cellist* (Tamar Levi), Spoleto. **Right:** Ciro Fodere at the piano

thought it logical to have history repeat itself, and I invited a large group of friends to Oscano to live like royalty for a few days—among the grand furnishings and lavish décor, the beautifully tiled floors and glorious views—and to attend a string of performances.

On the night of the Oscano concert, the audience was very excited, and the stage was set for a great performance in one of the castle's handsome outer buildings. On the program were Debussy, Stravinsky, Gershwin, Schubert, and MTT's own *Notturno*; the performance of this last would be an Italian premiere. The musicians had been somewhat nervous rehearsing with MTT that afternoon, although—as these were chamber concerts, not orchestra performances—he would not be with them onstage that night. Still, Michael's presence was more than enough to push them to be in absolutely top form.

If my initial fantasy was to hear beautiful music in a stunning setting, that dream was realized and surpassed with the Oscano concert. The weather was balmy, the sky a dense blue that deepened into night. Inside the stately hall, as the young performers—polished and dressed in elegant black tie—brought their attentions to the music, all rustling ceased in the audience. We sat mesmerized, listening, watching; the wafting tones of Debussy lulled us, the humor of Gershwin made us smile, and MTT's *Notturno* was the perfect and most intoxicating liquor for this evening.

More performances were arranged for the following day. On the guests' gold-embossed invitations, we had mischievously promised a "Mystery Concert." The audience members climbed onto the bus at Oscano in the morning, buzzing with curiosity—and some trepidation. Many of those attending were friends who, I well knew, are accustomed to making all their own decisions and are not used to mysteries, but in the end everyone good-naturedly played along, and the bus hummed down the *autostrada* toward our next venue: La Scarzuola.

During my scouting trip several months earlier, following a lead offered by Piero Colonna, I found myself on a road in what seemed the middle of nowhere, near the towns of Montegabbione and Montegiove, northeast of Orvieto. I nearly missed an inconspicuous road sign pointing downhill toward "Santa Maria della Scarzuola"—a

The Strings' Plot, San Terenziano, near Todi

55 *Trio* (Marilyn de Oliveira, Alice Dade, Yumiko Endo Schlaffer), near Perugia

typical Umbrian *strada bianca*, or dirt road, which was ragged, narrow, and winding through the foliage. The car tires threw up great clouds of dust as we drove down it. Finally we came to a stop in front of a tall wooden gate in a stone wall. We pulled a rope by the gate, ringing a distant bell, and were soon greeted by Brian Pentland, a very congenial Australian who welcomed us and, as he showed us around, recounted the fascinating story of this place.

Santa Maria della Scarzuola was the site of a monastery founded by the followers of St. Francis. It is said that in the early 1200s, at some point during his endless perambulations around Italy, the saint stopped at this spot, where he caused a bubbling spring to arise and built a shelter for himself out of *scarza,* a marsh reed that still grows on these grounds and that gives the place its name. The church and monastery were later built on the site. Brian opened the doors of the church for us, and inside we marveled at what is said to be one of the earliest pictures of St. Francis levitating.

But La Scarzuola has a far stranger and more secular side, too, which tends to upstage the ecclesiastic. After we left the church, Brian led us through a series of neatly structured gardens that opened suddenly onto the most extraordinary sight: spread out in front of us, cascading downward, was a full-scale amphitheater made of sand-colored tufa. Bundled at its side were midsize models of some of the most famous buildings in the world—the Acropolis, the Parthenon, the Pantheon, and more—all constructed of tufa. This was my first glimpse of the elaborate folly known as the Città Buzziana, named for its visionary creator, architect Tommaso Buzzi, who toiled at this mad and fantastical project over a period of three decades, beginning in the late 1950s. There is one surprise after another distributed around the grounds of La Scarzuola: gargoyles, reflecting pools, a giant stone whale with an open mouth big enough to walk into, a glass pyramid that houses a musical staircase (each step sounds a different musical tone), a house-sized stone torso of a naked woman, a temple devoted to Eros. The main amphitheater is only one of seven performance spaces in Buzzi's unfathomable plan, among them the "Teatro delle

ST. FRANCIS AND THE BIRDS

Italy's patron saint, Francis, is perhaps Umbria's most famous local figure. Born in Assisi in 1181 or 1182, he was the son of a well-to-do cloth merchant but renounced all material goods to embrace a life of extreme poverty and absolute faith. An itinerant soul, the saint traveled throughout Italy, both alone and in the company of disciples. Umbria is filled with Franciscan sites: from the glorious basilica at Assisi (which houses frescoes illustrating the life and miracles of the saint by Cimabue, Giotto, Simone Martini, Pietro Lorenzetti, and others) to the rustic *capella* on the Isola Maggiore in the middle of Lake Trasimeno, where Francis is reported to have spent a long Lenten period in the early thirteenth century. The ancient church at La Scarzuola boasts one of the oldest depictions of the saint miraculously levitating.

One of the best-known episodes of Francis's life—rendered by visual artists, filmmakers, composers, and writers alike—is his sermon to the birds. The saint's faith was such that he exhorted all animals to extend their gratitude to Heaven for their lives: "Oh birds, my brothers and sisters," he told them, "you have a great obligation to praise your Creator, who clothed you in feathers and gave you wings to fly with, provided you with pure air, and cares for you without any worry on your part." According to legend, the birds gathered lovingly around the saint and listened.

This was not the first time that the birds of Umbria had been invoked in a religious rite. More than a millennium earlier—before Christ, before the Roman conquests—a group of Jupiter-worshipping priests near ancient Iguvium (today's Gubbio) were instructed in the steps of a holy ritual: "Begin this ceremony by observing birds, those in front and those behind." The words are inscribed on the famous Eugubian Tables, seven bronze slabs that provide a crucial key to the language and culture of ancient Umbria. Today housed in the chapel of Gubbio's Palazzo dei Consoli, the tables are inscribed in the Umbrian language (written in both the Etruscan and the Latin alphabets), and offer invaluable evidence of the early life of this region.

In Umbria's lean and unyielding winter months, starlings gather in uncanny clouds over the wheat fields, their dotted masses creating pictographs in the sky. If you find yourself in a house with a view over distant hills—which in Umbria is a likely scenario—you may spend an afternoon marveling at the shapes made by their unified mass and wondering how in the world they know how to make them, and why. It is easy to see why St. Francis, and the pagan priests before him, sought spiritual connection through Umbria's winged fauna.

This page, top: Rehearsal, La Scarzuola. **Bottom:** MTT and musicians, Villa Colonna, near Orvieto. **Opposite:** MTT, Adam Zeichner, and Ciro Fodere offer the musicians

protection from the sun, La Scarzuola

Api" (Theater of Bees), the "Teatro delle Acque" (Theater of Water, where performances are reflected in a pool), a miniature theater space that grandly seats an audience of six, and a sloping esplanade of grass that was intended as the largest theater of them all.

Buzzi was far from finished with his project when he died in 1981, and the work of completion fell to his nephew and heir, Marco Solari, who, together with Brian, today runs La Scarzuola and is responsible for its daunting upkeep. I was enchanted by this very unusual place, and of course decided that the New World Symphony musicians must play here—the theater spaces of the Città Buzziana were crying out to be used. Brian and Marco graciously agreed to let us hold our "Mystery Concert" here.

On the day of the performance, our guests arrived at the gate of La Scarzuola and everyone dusted themselves off after their bumpy ride. Brian led them to the main amphitheater, where clarinetist Robert Woolfrey, violinists Daniel Carlson and Jennifer Best, violist Doyle Armbrust, and cellist Marilyn de Oliveira were playing Mozart's Clarinet Quintet on the lower floor of the theater. Hovering over them with umbrellas to protect the instruments from the harsh sun were MTT, Ciro Fodere, and Adam Zeichner. As the final Allegretto movement ended—before the spell could be broken—the audience was surprised by the ethereal strains of Debussy's *Syrinx* floating down to us from above: flutist Alice Dade was perched against the blue sky on one of the upper structures of the Città Buzziana. It was truly a moment of awe; the audience was perfectly silent as the last tones rang gently out.

We had planned this event as a "moveable feast"—a wandering concert, to explore the full spectrum of Buzzi's creation. After Alice's beautiful solo, we meandered to another spot to sip champagne while listening to Handel-Halvorsen's stately Passacaglia for Violin and Cello. The magic was that the audience heard the music, but the musicians— Jennifer and Marilyn—were hidden until they came out from the tiny six-seat theater to take their bows in front of a wide pool.

Perhaps the most moving concert of the day for me was the one that took place after lunch, in La Scarzuola's ancient little church. Ravel's

Sonatine for Flute, Viola, and Harp was performed by Alice and Doyle, with Yumiko Endo Schlaffer on the harp. Hearing them play that day was unforgettable; even now when I hear that particular Ravel piece, I am reminded that music—although I still know so little about it—is one manifestation of a higher meaning in this world.

The day was not over yet. That evening, we partook in an extraordinary dinner and concert at the Villa Aureli in Castel del Piano, outside Perugia. A lovely private estate belonging to Sperello and Carla di Serego Alighieri, the Villa Aureli is a sixteenth-century palazzo whose grounds are dotted with holm oaks and lemon trees, and surrounded by stone walls—and in whose gardens we gathered for the evening's events.

The brilliant chef Rodolfo Mencarelli, of Gubbio's Taverna del Lupo, had served us a magnificent buffet lunch at La Scarzuola, and then dashed off to Castel del Piano to prepare our evening meal. The menu that night was exquisite: we enjoyed veal carpaccio, *passatelli* pasta with truffle sauce in baskets of *parmigiano*, followed by pheasant with juniper sauce. The banquet ended with a gorgeous variety of delicate cakes and tortes and other *dolci*. Piero Colonna was my consultant in choosing the Umbrian wines for the events of the day, and it was a delight getting to know these gems. That night we savored the lovely Terre Vineate and a superb Lungarotti San Giorgio, with Decugnano dei Barbi's Spumante Brut for sparkle.

Although the wine had warmed us, the evening was rather chilly—and getting steadily colder—as we sat in our seats for the performance. We had arranged heaters around the grounds, but as Brahms's Piano Quartet started, our guests were shifting about in their seats, tightening their summer shawls, and shivering. The pianist Ciro Fodere noticed this and made an executive decision. Although there is a well-known principle in chamber music that the pianist must resist the temptation to overpower the other instruments, Ciro knew that somehow he had to warm up this crowd. As the quartet—made up of Ciro, Doyle on viola, Marilyn on cello, and Dan Carlson on violin—embarked on the last movement of the quartet, as Ciro recalls, "The only thing I could come up with was . . . to go *all the way*, and I did." He took the ball and ran: the piano part

shimmered with intensity. "Thanks to my colleagues' amazing musicianship and personalities," Ciro notes gently, "nobody was offended." In fact, the audience became so involved with the energy of the music that the chill did seem to be dispelled—and despite the perhaps unorthodox performance, MTT praised the quartet for a wonderful job.

After that triumphant final concert of the day, our group made its way back to the Castello dell'Oscano. And the next morning, like campers who have formed a bond having shared life-changing experiences, the guests weepily said good-bye and promised to stay in touch. I hope—I believe—that the confluence of Umbria and music did constitute a life-changing experience for everyone. It certainly did for me.

Shortly after our extraordinary day of "Mystery Concerts," I returned to the Villa Aureli with Neil and his crew to shoot still lifes in the house and gardens.

I would have the good fortune later on to befriend Carla and Sperello di Serego Alighieri, but it was clear on this day that Sperello—although he had greatly enjoyed our concert in the garden—was somewhat nervous to see his home invaded by a team of strangers bearing a truckload of photo equipment, as well as assorted musical instruments, fruits and vegetables, animal carcasses, several dead fish, lobsters, octopi, and one live tortoise.

The Villa Aureli has been in the Alighieri family for several generations and has an extremely interesting history. The oldest part of the villa dates back to the 1500s, but the building was expanded and remodeled over the course of the following centuries. The extant details tell some of its story: eighteenth-century frescoes adorn a number of ceilings, and much of the villa's furniture dates from the same period; lovely balconies were added to the second-story windows in the late nineteenth century; and many of the floors are covered with

THE UMBRIA FILM FESTIVAL

What is more magical than an outdoor movie? In the summertime, many Umbrian towns screen classic films in parks or at historic sites—from Perugia's Giardini del Frontone and Città di Castello's CDCinema to Castiglione del Lago's Palazzo della Corgna, where the screen is set against the sparkling backdrop of Lake Trasimeno. Somewhat more edgy is the Umbria Film Festival, which takes place each July in the town of Montone, in the region's upper Tiber Valley.

The festival is the brainchild of acclaimed director Terry Gilliam, whose films include *Jabberwocky*, *Brazil*, *Twelve Monkeys*, and most recently *The Imaginarium of Dr. Parnassus*, and who is also well known for his long association with the Monty Python troupe. Gilliam has a residence near Montone and helped launch the Umbria Film Festival in 1995. It has been going strong ever since, showcasing movies by filmmakers from all over the world.

Montone is like many Umbrian villages: perched on a beautiful hilltop, surrounded by imposing stone walls, and made up primarily of well-kept stone alleys, stairways, and houses with tiled roofs and bright geraniums overflowing from windowsills. The views from upper stories are breathtaking, and the central square—Piazza Fortebraccio, named for the town's most famous resident, the powerful fourteenth-century condottiere Braccio Fortebraccio—is a charming gathering place dotted with small cafés.

Darkness does not fall on Italian summer nights until after ten o'clock. The heat of the day abates, giving way to a clear and lovely evening warmth. People find one another at bars and cafés and drink *digestivi* or cool *spremute* (freshly pressed fruit juices). Chairs are set up throughout the piazza and a state-of-the-art screen is stretched between two buildings. The feature film is preceded by screenings of several short movies for children, which are judged by a panel—of children—who soberly mark down their preferences on slips of paper. (This is, incidentally, currently the only competitive aspect of the festival, but it is nonetheless a serious matter, as is evident in the stern expressions on the faces of the young judges.) As the children's movies cannot begin before dark (and tend to start even later), the main film may not go on until midnight or so.

The Umbria Film Festival includes both feature-length and short films in genres that range across the board, from comedy, fantasy, and horror to drama and documentary. In recent years the festival has hosted "Umbriametraggi"—a section of the event devoted solely to filmmakers born or living in Umbria. Over the years, the Umbria Film Festival has included screenings of Ken Loach's *The Wind that Shakes the Barley*, Bahman Ghobadi's *Half Moon*, Lone Scherfig's *An Education*, and Gilliam's own delightful tale of the mythical Baron Munchausen. Gilliam himself describes this last event evocatively:

Floating high above an eternal landscape, in the heart of a dark stone town, images from The Adventures of Baron Munchausen *tumble across a giant screen which towers over a small moonlit square. While children play, people sitting at tables or chairs arranged as an alfresco cinema, chat, talk, watch—captured by the film.*

Cinema sotto le stelle: cinema beneath the stars—a very memorable way to spend an evening in Umbria.

Villa Aureli, Castel del Piano

colorful ceramic tiles from Naples that were installed in the early twentieth century. During World War II, the building was used as the local headquarters of the German Army, and later of the Allied Forces. The precious furnishings that are here today were preserved during the war by a faithful and heroic gardener, who hurriedly constructed false walls in the villa and secreted the furniture into these hidden rooms before the house was overtaken. Thankfully, the villa itself suffered little damage during its occupation.

When Sperello, who has a successful career as an astrophysicist, inherited the estate from his father a few years ago, it created something of an upheaval in his life. The property is magnificent, but requires constant attention and care—attention that Sperello once reserved for the stars. He and Carla live in the villa's downstairs rooms, and rent out suites in the upper stories, as well as two outer buildings. They are a very charming and cultivated couple, and although the work on the villa and surrounding land is never-ending, they seem to take it very much in stride. Sheep graze peacefully in their distant meadow, and there is a sense of calm on the Villa Aureli's grounds.

The family's history is at least as intriguing as the villa's. The name Alighieri carries vast weight: Sperello is a descendant of the poet Dante Alighieri. (The couple kindly gave me a bottle of the delicious red wine Vaio Armaron, produced by Sperello's cousin in the Valpolicella region— on land that has been in the family since Dante's son Pietro bought it in 1353.) Another ancestor was the celebrated explorer Pietro Savorgnan di Brazzà, for whom Congo's Brazzaville was named. Carla and Sperello's son, Pietro, is a student of his forebear's work; he has traveled extensively in Africa, and recently collaborated on a documentary film titled *The Weak Current*, about Brazzà's legacy in today's troubled Congo. When I visited the family at a later time, Sperello showed me photographs of a motorcycle trip he had taken from Perugia to Beijing, and he and Carla spoke animatedly about an extraordinary trek they had recently made, also by motorcycle, throughout Patagonia.

I suppose I was a bit surprised to encounter such adventurous and dauntless people in Umbria, where the inhabitants seem so rooted in their home and traditions. In the nearby town of Solomeo, I learned of another Umbrian who didn't fit the mold I'd constructed: the cashmere manufacturer Brunello Cucinelli, who travels to the far corners of the planet in quest of the very finest wools. And Sarah di Belmonte introduced me to still another unexpected local character who helped me greatly in getting to know the region: Il Conte Giuseppe Vicarelli Saluzzo di Monterosso e di Valgrana—far more commonly known as "Bepi."

Bepi derives from an old and well-respected Umbrian family. His mother, Luisa Alpina Manzoni Vicarelli, was the initial driving force behind making Perugia the "sister city" of Seattle, Washington, and Bepi has taken up the mantle of that endeavor with much energy. His aunt, Rosetta Ansidei di Catrano, is a well-loved but somewhat formidable figure in Perugia; at one point I had the opportunity to observe a ceremony of the Knights of Malta, and I noted that the other attendants bowed and curtsied to Rosetta as she passed them with an air of great majesty. Bepi, on the other hand, has little truck with ceremony—though he does have an occasional taste for flourish. One day you might see him at a tony café in Perugia, or zipping about in his adored Jaguar, sporting a rakish suede hunting jacket and fedora with a pheasant feather in its brim—and the next day find him in an old undershirt, shorts, and tennis shoes, having just spent hours with his young son, Giulio, gathering grapes from the vineyard on his estate.

Bepi is, in some ways, a classic Umbrian: he works tremendously hard and loves his land profoundly. When I first met him in 2005, he had just finished restoring his small castle, Montecapanno, which had been badly damaged in a 1997 earthquake. The epicenter had been in the nearby town of Foligno; the quake killed a dozen people and destroyed many buildings in the area. Particularly devastated was the town of Assisi, where four people lost their lives and several precious frescoes were shattered when the ceiling of the famous Basilica di San Francesco collapsed. The frescoes—by Giotto, Cimabue, and others—have since been restored, but memories of the tragedy, and the lesson about nature's sometimes cruel powers, remain painful.

SOLOMEO AND BRUNELLO CUCINELLI

Umbria is known and loved for what is often termed its "earthiness": its remarkable lack of gilding and pomp. Although it is scattered with breathtaking castles, villas, cathedrals, and fortresses, the region's greatest allure is the mountainous green landscape. So it comes as something of a surprise that one of Italy's most elegant and luxurious commodities is produced in Umbria: the exquisite cashmeres of Brunello Cucinelli.

Cucinelli, a very dapper man in his fifties, was born to a farming family in the Umbrian town of Castel Rigone. He worked the land until he was a teenager, and then moved with his parents to the outskirts of Perugia, where his father took a job in a factory. In the late 1970s, the young Cucinelli started the company that would eventually grow to be one of the top-ranking cashmere manufacturers in the world.

Despite the sumptuousness of his products, Cucinelli maintains a typically Umbrian, down-to-earth, "humanistic" philosophy when it comes to his business. In 1985 he purchased a castle in the fourteenth-century village of Solomeo, near Perugia; over the subsequent years, he bought and restored the entire village, installing his company headquarters and manufacturing facilities in its lovely, ancient stone buildings. Today, Solomeo seems to be not so much a town as a beautiful workplace: its few tiny streets are empty, and a peek into the windows of the stone buildings reveals men and women busy working at tables and machines, bundles of wool culled from Mongolian goats, and swaths of knitted fabrics in the subtlest colors.

Cucinelli, who has famously stated that his heroes are Socrates, Seneca, and his fellow Umbrians St. Benedict and St. Francis, feels strongly that his employees are his collaborators. "Everyone who works for me has the key to the premises," Cucinelli says. "They come and go when they want and no one has to clock in. . . . They work as if they were at home." He believes in a modern form of capitalism that serves the betterment of humankind: "All my life I have followed one dream," he says, "to make work more human."

In 2008 he opened a small theater in Solomeo: the Teatro Cucinelli. The company's idealistic president hopes with this to inspire a true "forum of the arts" for the twenty-first century—"a place," he says, "where people can talk." Solomeo also houses a boutique of Cucinelli products. Here, visitors may attempt to resist the irresistible cashmeres for sale by leafing through a photo album showing the company's founder in Mongolia with the goats who provide this exquisite wool. Although Cucinelli seldom travels to Asia these days, his vision is still clearly global, as well as firmly local.

Bepi's reconstructed Castellina di Montecapanno is, however, one beautiful consolation. Neil was charmed by the place and set up a marvelous picture on the property. Inspired by Caravaggio's *Rest on the Flight into Egypt*, he positioned Alice Dade with her flute, Dan Carlson with his violin, and Bepi, seated, holding out a book of music with one hand and the harness of his son's pony, Pippo, with the other. (To Bepi's consternation, a makeup artist strummed lines onto his face to make him look older than he is—in keeping with Caravaggio's vision—but he was mollified when he finally saw the resulting photograph.)

Bepi wanted very much to show me around the Università di Perugia. Founded in 1308, this is one of the oldest universities in the world—and Bepi's own ancestor Bartolo Alfani da Sassoferrato was an important and influential figure on its law school faculty in the fourteenth century. While many of the university's main buildings are on the via Fabretti, in what was once an Olivetan monastery, the campus is spread out throughout the city.

We visited the impressive Biblioteca del Dottorato (doctoral library), whose director, Gianfranco Cialini, told us of a remarkable recent discovery. While taking inventory of the *biblioteca's* holdings, the library staff found a previously unknown, fully intact musical parchment, as well as fragments of some ten other musical pieces, all dating from the mid-fourteenth century. The discovery of these fragments of polyphonic music sheds new light on the study of the music of this era, the so-called *ars nova*.

Bepi seems to know and be known by everyone in Umbria. He once told me that he and the mayor of Perugia made a lighthearted wager about which of them was more famous. Bepi won the bet hands-down by showing the mayor a postcard from the United States that had been successfully delivered to his home, though it was addressed simply to "BEPI, PERUGIA, ITALIA." He loves meeting new friends and making connections, and he takes great pleasure in introducing people to one another.

Bepi introduced me to his friends Carlo and Alessandra Sorbello and persuaded them to invite us for lunch at their home near Umbertide.

At the Biblioteca del Dottorato, Università di Perugia (Gianfranco Cialini at right)

After Caravaggio's "Rest on the Flight into Egypt" (Bepi Vicarelli, Alice Dade, Dan Carlson),

Castellina di Montecapanno

The Castello di Sorbello is a massive, tenth-century fortress hidden deep in a thick forest—but its owners are as friendly and down-to-earth as the castle is imposing. Carlo and Alessandra greeted Bepi and me and led us up a wide staircase of white marble and through what was once the *salone di giustizia* (hall of justice), ending in a cozy study; there we sat on comfortable leather sofas while Carlo told us some of the history of the *castello*, which has remained in his family for ten eventful centuries. Due to its strategic location on the border between the Papal States and the Grand Duchy of Tuscany, the Castello di Sorbello was for much of its history used as a military base. Today, its isolated location, surrounded by a sea of trees, gives the castle an atmosphere of great peace and calm.

We had lunch in the Sorbellos' light-filled dining room and continued to chat. As we ate, I noticed that beneath our plates were beautiful, very unusual embroidered placemats, and I asked Carlo and Alessandra where they were from. Like everything else at the Castello di Sorbello, they have a history. Carlo had an American grandmother named Romeyne Robert, who met and married his grandfather, Ruggero Ranieri di Sorbello, in the early twentieth century. Romeyne took an interest in reviving and revalorizing local artisanal traditions, and in 1904 she founded the Scuola del Pischiello, an embroidery school that was based in Passignano, near Lake Trasimeno. There, young women of need were taught the exacting techniques of embroidery—including the *punto umbro* or *portoghese* stitch, which is now known as the *punto Sorbello*: this is the raised, knotlike stitch I had been admiring on Carlo and Alessandra's placemats. Though the school is no longer in existence, a number of its embroidered pieces can be admired today at New York's Cooper-Hewitt Museum or at the Uguccione Ranieri di Sorbello Foundation in Perugia.

The Sorbellos attended several of our chamber concerts in Umbria, and clearly enjoyed them—which makes me very happy. What began as a lovely luncheon has now developed into a warm and ongoing friendship.

Piero and Andrée di Colonna too have become good friends. As longtime residents, they were also invaluable as guides to lesser-known parts of Umbria. The Colonnas' stone villa near Orvieto is warm, elegant, and unpretentious. A bounty of geraniums surrounds the entranceway to their home, and when I visited, their two Jack Russell terriers, Arturo and Sheila, greeted me with a great deal of doggish enthusiasm and charm.

In the garden behind the house, the Colonnas have artfully cut an opening in the foliage to allow a view directly onto Orvieto's *duomo*, just across the valley. Andrée confided to me that she had long had a wild fantasy of bringing a grand piano to this magical spot and listening to a performance while gazing at the vista. I thought this was a spectacular idea—and we arranged for our production crew to bring in a piano, which MTT obligingly played while the other musicians gathered around him. Neil encouraged us to carry the fun even further, posing musicians and members of the production crew as figures from Botticelli's *Primavera*—with Piero, Andrée, and me cast as three unwitting Graces, observing the scene from the sidelines.

After the shoot at the Colonnas', MTT and I drove into Orvieto, which sits on a high tufa outcrop that rises like a thick pancake from the valley below.

At the center of the city is the glorious cathedral, whose façade—crowded with mosaics, statuary, bas-reliefs, pilasters, and arches—is famed throughout the world as a stunning example of Italian Gothic workmanship. MTT wanted to show me the cathedral's famous Cappella della Madonna di San Brizio. Although I had been to the *duomo* before, I had never entered this side chapel, which holds one of the great treasures of Italy: the fresco cycle depicting the end of the world and the aftermath of Judgment Day by Luca Signorelli. The chapel's walls seem to throb with life. Signorelli's rendition of *The Damned* is particularly

After Botticelli's "Primavera,"
78 Villa Colonna, near Orvieto

vivid: a tangle of unhappy naked bodies in various states of torment, including, at the center, a young woman who looks up despairingly toward the heavenly archangels as she is dragged off on the back of a winged demon. We were transfixed by the paintings and stayed until our craning necks could take it no more.

Orvieto became a favorite haunt, and I came to know many of its corners. The city's origins date back to the Iron Age, and an important Etruscan township called Velzna existed on this site in the ninth century B.C. Today's city is underrun by a labyrinth of old caves that shoot through the tufa—a visit to these can provide a cool respite on a stifling Italian afternoon. A funicular runs between the upper town and its lower outskirts; near its entrance is the Pozzo di San Patrizio, built in the sixteenth century by Antonio Sangallo the Younger. It is an extraordinary feat of architecture: a 203-foot-deep well designed to provide an emergency water supply to the city in case of siege.

My visits to Orvieto nearly always included a stop at the Vinosus wine bar and restaurant in the Piazza del Duomo (where I discovered perhaps my favorite Umbrian white wine, Antinori's Cervaro della Sala) and at the *gelateria* next door, which makes what I consider to be the best Baci-flavored gelato in all of Italy. I also love the Bottega Michelangeli, which is near the Torre del Moro (Moor's tower) in the center of town. I found it one day as I walked along the central Corso Cavour: caught by the sight of a wooden doll staring out at me through a shop window, I entered and discovered a world of exquisite hand-carved wooden figures, ornaments, and furnishings. The shop was opened by the late Gualverio Michelangeli, a fifth-generation wood-carver whose creations were known around the world; today, the business is run by his daughters, Donatella, Raffaella, and Simonetta. In Neil's photograph of a little girl with feathered white wings—I think of her as the Spirit of Umbria—a Michelangeli angel hovers in the background.

I loved showing the young musicians around the region, which was entirely new to most of them (Doyle Armbrust admitted later that he wasn't sure he had even *heard* of Umbria before this trip).

I brought them to the Falsettini-Forenza stained-glass studio in Perugia, where Neil photographed several of them with their instruments among the glass pieces. We went to vineyards and olive-oil manufacturers, whose owners are staunchly proud of their products, which—they reminded us—have been around for millennia with relatively little change in the production process. We visited the Temple of Clitunno, near Trevi, and at the nearby Taverna del Pescatore we ate fish that had been caught just minutes before. And the musicians and I visited the Lungarottis' Poggio alle Vigne, where Neil made a beautiful still life of glistening grapes.

Discovering new delights in food was a central part of the experience for many of the young people: when I later asked them what they remembered most vividly about Umbria, this was always somewhere near the top of the list. "The food, oh the food!" Marilyn de Oliveira rhapsodized. Flutist Ebonee Thomas (who traveled with us in 2006) said, "I didn't know food could taste that good. It was as if everything was made with love, care, pride, and passion. I have become a food snob. . . . After eating such fresh, good-quality, and beautiful meals, I feel I don't have to settle for just anything!"

I experience a great thrill when I hear, see, try something wonderful for the first time, as well as when I watch another person respond with joy and amazement to something new. I had such thrills many times over during this Umbria project.

LUCA SIGNORELLI AND THE ORVIETO CHAPEL

Umbria is well-punctuated with works by the great Renaissance painter Luca Signorelli, whose pivotal role in the trajectory of Italian art history is undisputed. From the tiny town of Morra, whose Oratorio di San Crescentino houses the artist's chilling scene of the *Flagellation of Christ*, to Citerna's *Madonna and Child with Sts. Michael and Francis and Two Angels*, to Città di Castello's *Martyrdom of St. Sebastian*, Signorelli's hand left traces in this region that alone would make a pilgrimage to Umbria worthwhile.

Born around 1445 in the Tuscan town of Cortona, near the Umbrian border, Signorelli was influenced by the great master Piero della Francesca, with whom he is said to have apprenticed as a young man. He traveled to Rome in the late 1470s; there he completed several works, including a fresco for the Sistine Chapel. He also worked in Città di Castello, where he must have been well-loved: he was proclaimed a citizen of the city in 1488. Numerous pieces by Signorelli may be seen in his hometown of Cortona as well, and his frescoes at Monte Oliveto Maggiore, near Siena—depicting the life of St. Benedict of Norcia—are breathtaking, though badly damaged.

But it is Signorelli's fresco cycle in the Cappella della Madonna di San Brizio in Orvieto that is unquestionably his masterpiece. The commission for the chapel's murals went initially to Fra Angelico, who completed a number of images in the vaults over the altar before breaking his contract in 1447 and moving on to other commissions. The *duomo*'s administrators then spent several decades wooing other artists (including Umbria's golden son, Perugino) to finish the fresco cycle. Ultimately, it was Signorelli who took up the completion of the job, some fifty years after Angelico's start.

Signorelli's extraordinary scenes of damnation and salvation—works fully charged with motion and emotion, raw physicality and ethereal light—were apparently studied by Michelangelo before he set to work at the Sistine Chapel. The cycle follows the narrative of the biblical Last Judgment, beginning with *The Preaching of the Antichrist*—a scene that is very rarely encountered in major works of art. In one corner of this depiction of the false prophet, Signorelli includes portraits of Fra Angelico and of himself (Signorelli looks slyly out at the viewer, making contact with us through the centuries). Above the chapel's entrance arch is the dramatic *End of the World*, after which cataclysm of course comes the division of humanity into saved and damned. The next scene, *The Resurrection of the Dead*, shows hordes of thick-muscled humans rising out of the ground and gazing beatifically up at the angels who beckon them heavenward with golden trumpets. But—as we see in the next scene—there is an alternative ending. *Heaven and Hell* shows, on the left, glorious seraphim welcoming virtuous humans to Paradise; on the right, stern angels oversee demons as they transport sinners to fiery Hell.

It may be a sin to admire *The Damned*, but this scene is truly the highlight of the cycle. Here, a mass of fleshy human figures, doomed to eternal punishment, is swarmed by green-tinted flying devils, come to collect the souls that are their due. Over the crowd preside sword-wielding archangels who look somberly down at this scene of torture and lamentation. Opposite this powerful fresco is *The Coronation of the Elect*. Here again, Signorelli indulges his great talents as a painter of the human body (although in this group, genitals are covered with strategically draped cloths). Now located safely in Paradise, these figures look joyfully toward loved ones with whom they are at last reunited, or thankfully toward the orchestra of musical angels that floats above them.

Every inch of the San Brizio chapel is filled with dazzling imagery: Fra Angelico's *Christ in Majesty* looks down from his throne in an upper vault, and the spaces between Signorelli's frescoes are painted with faux architectural details that encapsulate fanciful grotesques as well as portraits—including renditions of Dante, Cicero, and Virgil. The chapel's walls are alive with color and energy, and visitors are inevitably left considering the perennially meaningful themes of life, death, *Paradiso*, and *Inferno*.

Thanks to Piero and Andrée, we were offered access to one of Umbria's most beautiful private gardens.

The Colonnas' neighbor and friend Mila Brachetti Peretti agreed to feature a concert at her annual June *festa* celebrating the extraordinary roses on the grounds of her estate near Orvieto. Mila's gardens were designed by acclaimed landscape architect Paolo Pejrone, and to see them at the peak of bloom was truly awe-inspiring: "Sea Foam" white roses spilled over colossal cast-iron flower baskets; "Sally Holmes" roses cascaded down from around boxwood hedges—everywhere roses and other flowers poured forth joyfully.

At the Brachetti Peretti home, Neil was inspired to pose MTT, Doyle Armbrust, and Alice Dade on the grass in a charming echo of Manet's *Déjeuner sur l'herbe*, with Yumiko Endo Schlaffer strumming the harp in the background. Later, Alice would confide in me that this particular photo shoot was extremely difficult for her—she had never set out to be a model, after all, and holding one position for so long can be painful. It was so painful, in fact, that at dinner that evening, to her own mortification, she burst into tears in front of MTT. But this experience and the rest of her time in Italy were in the end very important for Alice: "I was so tightly bound before my first step in Italy!" she recently told me. "I wanted all my ducks in a row, all the control. But, as I've figured out, life just isn't that way. And since I've figured that out . . . it's so much *fun!*" Letting go of rules can be a difficult lesson for a talented and disciplined young musician.

The concert that took place in Mila's garden was the perfect synthesis of elements: the luxurious abundance and scent of the flowers, the pristine skies of a June day, and the electrifying music. Somehow, Vivaldi's Piccolo Concerto in C Major seemed particularly well-suited to the moment: exultant Italian music in this unmistakably Italian setting. Mila had shown me a row of trees in one corner of her grounds that had been planted especially to attract birds—hearing Alice Dade on the piccolo that afternoon, I could only think that those birds must be so proud, listening to the vibrant voice of what was surely one of their kin.

Our 2005 series of Umbrian concerts came to a close in a very beautiful and touching way. It had been exactly a year since my friend Shirley Caraciollo's husband, François, had passed away. Shirley and her son, Riccardo, asked if the NWS musicians might perform a memorial concert at their villa at Monte Calvo, on the hills overlooking Todi. Just behind the house is the ruin of a tall stone tower; the ensemble of musicians was positioned at its base—again, a grand piano was rolled out for us—and as night came on, a bright moon rose directly over them. The music that evening—Mozart, Ravel, Debussy, and Schubert—seemed to take us to another plane; it was, I think, a deeply meaningful memorial event for François.

After the last of the concerts, the musicians busied themselves preparing for the return home and plans for the rest of the summer. Most of them were continuing with the New World Symphony, but a few—among them Doyle Armbrust, Jennifer Best, Marilyn de Oliveira, and David DeRiso—were at the end of their three-year stint with the academy and moving on to other positions. Musicians who play regularly together naturally form a kind of familial bond, but I believe that this trip to Umbria did even more to tighten the connections among these young people. They had shared an extraordinary few weeks, many experiencing for the first time such stunning landscapes, such sumptuous foods . . . and the musicians had in turn given so much of themselves. Umbria's generosity had been reflected back at it by these wonderful young people, and I was overjoyed to have had a hand in that reciprocity.

After Manet's "Le Déjeuner sur l'Herbe"
(Alice Dade, Doyle Armbrust, Yumiko Endo Schlaffer, MTT),
Villa Brachetti Peretti, near Orvieto

The following summer brought a new group of New World Symphony musicians to Umbria for another round of concerts and photo sessions with Neil Folberg.

Adam Zeichner again worked with Neil to select a group, and MTT created the musical programs.

This year our home base was Spoleto, one of Umbria's most cosmopolitan centers. The city is renowned for its Festival dei Due Mondi, or Festival of Two Worlds, which brings in hordes of visitors each July to attend music, dance, and other performances. Gian Carlo Menotti founded the festival in 1958, driven, as he said, by the need to convey to the general public "the usefulness and the necessity of artists." I find a statement of his to be particularly inspiring:

It takes patience to demonstrate that civilized man "lives" on art without even realizing it. The tune he whistles while shaving was composed by a musician, the newspaper he reads in the morning and the comedy he watches on TV in the evening were written by writers, the beautiful clothes his wife wears were indubitably created by a designer, as were the elegant silverware and china on his dinner table. . . . Stravinsky and Prokofiev emerge from sound tracks of box office hits for an audience that is repelled by talk of classical or contemporary music. In a word, for me the concept of the Festival has always been to get the artist to come down from his pedestal and mix with the public.

I admire Menotti's impulse to win over an audience trained by society to be "repelled" by classical and contemporary music. Somehow, over the course of the past two or three generations, much of the general public (perhaps especially in the United States) has come to feel that certain genres of music are foreign to them—reserved only for a small circle of people who have somehow amassed vast stores of knowledge about the subject. No wonder they are repelled; I, too, was turned off by classical music until I came to see that it does not need to be such a heady business. Indeed, I believe it is much more about the heart than the mind—or that the mind *follows* the heart into music, rather than the other way around.

Our group arrived in Spoleto in May 2006, a relatively quiet month in that lovely city. We all stayed at the Hotel San Luca, at the base of the hill upon which Spoleto is built. The hotel's owners are Daniela and Paolo Zuccari, who also run the Villa Zuccari outside the city, in nearby Montefalco. Their daughter, Federica, and her husband, Carlo, look after the San Luca, and made us feel truly part of the family while we were there. Federica was very pregnant when we arrived and during our stay she gave birth to a beautiful daughter, Claudia. We felt very welcomed by the Zuccaris, and—not wanting them to forget us—Neil took a photograph of the musicians, which we left in the *salone* of the San Luca, with the regards of the New World Symphony engraved on the silver frame.

Daniela Zuccari is one of those Italian women who are both extremely elegant and an absolute wizard in the kitchen. She oversees the teams of cooks at both hotels, and the NWS musicians were regularly stunned by the wonderful fare that appeared on their plates at breakfasts, lunches, and dinners in the San Luca dining room. Among the treats we looked forward to each morning were Daniela's *crostate*, thin tarts filled with berries, toasted almonds, marmalade, or cream, some of them checkered on top with strips of sweet pastry. After a long day of rehearsals and photo shoots, the young musicians would sit down with sighs of happiness to comforting bowls of garlicky *zuppa di fave*—one of Umbria's signature dishes, made with puréed fava beans—with puddles of dark-green olive oil from a local *fabbrica* drizzled on top. There could be nothing more sustaining for our hardworking young artists.

Spoleto is a great walking city, and we roamed every inch of it, from the well-preserved Roman amphitheater to the Mascherone fountain with its grotesque monster-face in the Piazza Campello, from the busy market streets of the central town to the Rocca Albornoziana, the imposing fortress at the summit of the Spoleto hill. A number of the NWS

THE UMBRIAN MORNING

For most of the year, Umbria is hot enough in the middle of the day to warrant a break from work—particularly for folks whose vocations keep them outdoors, which is a large portion of Umbria's agriculture-driven population. To make up for the loss of those siesta hours, Umbrians tend to begin their workday early. Breakfast is simple and generally not heavy (as in most Mediterranean countries, in Italy the main meal is generally eaten at midday). Coffee is a necessity for most, whether a comforting *caffè latte* sipped from a bowl at home or a froth-coated cappuccino at the bar of a café, or for a real jolt with a built-in palliative, a *caffè corretto*—espresso "corrected" with a shot of grappa. For the child in all of us, the cafés of Città di Castello, in the northern part of the region, are famous for their *cioccolato caldo:* a dark hot chocolate so rich you have to eat it with a spoon.

Any of these beverages may be dunked with biscotti, which are small and often studded with almonds (also known as *cantuccini alle mandorle*). Several may be dropped into a bowl of *caffè latte* to round out the first meal of the day.

At the Hotel San Luca in Spoleto, breakfast is a delight: in a sun-drenched room dotted with neatly lain tables, visitors may help themselves from a banquet of fruits, *marmellate*, juices, and—best of all—homemade baked goods from the kitchen of Daniela Zuccari. Signora Zuccari was kind enough to share a recipe for her breakfast *crostata* (here amended slightly for the American kitchen). Simple and versatile, this tart may of course also serve as a delicate and wonderful dessert.

Crostata
Makes two 8- to 10-inch tarts

The *crostata* should be thin and shallow—like a pizza—not deep like a pie.

Ingredients
1 whole egg and 2 yolks
3/4 cup sugar
4 ounces (1 stick) butter,
    melted and cooled
2 cups flour
1/2 teaspoon salt (optional)
3/4 to 1 cup marmalade or jam
Pine nuts, slivered almonds, and/or sliced apple (optional)

Preheat oven to 350 degrees F. Butter two 8-inch pie tins or 10-inch flat pizza pans (Daniela Zuccari uses soft silicone pans).

In a bowl, mix together with a wooden spoon egg, yolks, and sugar. (Signora Zuccari advises: "Count to thirty as you mix.") Add the cooled melted butter. Sift flour (and salt, if using) and add to the bowl slowly. When the mixture is soft and sticky, mix gently until it is of a uniform consistency.

Divide the dough in two and pat gently into the two baking tins—working it as little as possible, yet making it as thin as possible. (The dough should be pressed into place with the palm of the hand and your fingers; overworking it will result in a tough crust.) Let it rest for 30 minutes in the refrigerator.

Spoon half the marmalade into each of the two tart bases. Spread it evenly, leaving a 1/2-inch ring of exposed dough around the edge. If desired, sprinkle the tarts with pine nuts, slivered almonds, and/or thinly sliced apple.

Bake for about 18 minutes, or until the crust around the edge is golden and the marmalade is hot and beginning to bubble.

Serve warm or at room temperature, preferably accompanied by warm *caffè latte* (at breakfast) or followed by espresso (after dinner).

92   Lorenzo Padrichelli, Andra Lunde, and their baby, David

musicians are devoted joggers, and they discovered a beautiful route that took them straight over the Ponte delle Torri—the very tall Roman aqueduct and bridge that runs from La Rocca to Monteluco on the other side of the valley. Violinist Jerome Gordon recalls stealing a few moments for himself in Spoleto, "wandering the *piazze*, running in the hills and along the aqueduct. . . . These experiences left indelible memories and were some of the most personal encounters I had with Umbria."

All the musicians fell in love with the Osteria del Trivio, a small nook around the corner from the Hotel San Luca. In true "osteria" fashion, the fare is traditional and uncomplicated, but perfectly executed, from gnocchi and hand-cut pastas to stuffed artichokes, stewed lentils, sautéed *sanguinosi* (blood-red wild mushrooms), roast boar—and all ending, if anyone still has room, with the delectable *crescionda*, a distinctly Umbrian confection made with crushed *amaretti*, chocolate, and cream. Needless to say, we became fast friends with the restaurant's owners, Umberto and Mirella Muraro: one of the musicians, Dustin Budish, fondly recalls that we received a loud and hearty greeting every time we entered the establishment.

One always seems to discover a feeling of kinship, of *home*, in Umbria. I felt nourished myself seeing the young musicians find connections to Italy. They loved the leisurely evenings at cafés, chatting, flirting, enjoying the cool night air. Clarinetist Alucia Scalzo was excited to encounter a man in Spoleto who shared her last name. "I couldn't speak Italian, and Giuseppe Scalzo couldn't speak English," she says, "but after I showed him my driver's license, he gave me a huge hug and a kiss on each cheek. . . . It really felt like family." Some of the musicians took a day trip to Rome—only an hour or so away by train—but scurried back as quickly as they could, dejected. They had gone to lunch at a less-than-fabulous restaurant, had been overwhelmed and confused trying to navigate the traffic and the monuments, and generally felt like outsiders in the big city. They missed the warmth and easy welcome of Umbria.

I got to know the little shops along Spoleto's winding streets, which sell everything from jars of truffles to handwoven shawls and table linens to lovely perfumed soaps and hand creams. Rita Cammi, on

SAVORING AN UMBRIAN MEAL

The importance of food is made very clear at Il Castagneto, the *agriturismo* owned and run by Elsa and Luigi Palmerini, located near the town of Castiglione del Lago.

Elsa is a sweetly modest woman in her mid-forties, with practical, short blond hair and a kind, round face. She is nearly always seen in her utilitarian blue and white apron. Il Castagneto attracts both foreigners and Italians, including many locals who come by in the evenings to partake in the results of Elsa's celebrated culinary talents.

Elsa's kitchen is small, tidy, and efficiently set up for the task at hand, which always involves pasta, roasting meat, and baking. For tonight, Elsa is starting with *strangozzi*, the hearty, thick pasta typical of this area (and variously known as *pici* or *umbricelli*). In a concession to modern amenities, Elsa sometimes uses a crank pasta machine (her neighbors may raise their eyebrows at this "shortcut," but it does not stop them from eating her delicious food). *Strangozzi*, however, absolutely must be rolled out, cut, and shaped by hand. The dough is flattened slightly before a summary press with the palm to bring it into shape; then it is cut into rough lengths. She has already made the *ragù di cinghiale*, the boar sauce, through which the pasta will be gently drawn. In the wood stove are a dozen squab, roasting slowly until they are dark and succulent. The birds have been fed on good grain all their lives, which of course adds to their flavor. But Elsa warns: "It doesn't matter how good the pigeon is if you don't cook it right. It's very simple, but really it must be over wood, or it won't taste the same."

Inevitably, the meal begins with *crostini*: small toasts spread with a blend of sautéed chicken livers and capers, crushed together into a paste—or plain toasts served simply beside a small jug of aromatic olive oil, with pieces of cut garlic to rub on them. After the guests have enjoyed these *primi*, Luigi—a thin, lively man with quick eyes and a conspiratorial smile—goes from table to table in the dining room bearing a massive ceramic bowl from which he serves the *strangozzi al ragù*, and then refills glasses with hearty red wine, poured from a white pitcher. In the kitchen, Elsa dips zucchini and zucchini flowers into a thin batter of flour, milk, and egg, and then fries them quickly and suddenly in deep oil. She arranges the *piccioni* (pigeons) on a large platter and carefully places the vegetables and flowers around them.

Eating at the Palmerinis', an American visitor might mistakenly conclude that the word *basta* (enough) must mean "More, please": Luigi is infamously insistent on serving seconds, and even thirds. "*Grazie, basta,*" you might protest, covering your dish with a protective hand in the hope of saving room for the next several courses, but Luigi will simply lift his spoon over the obstruction and continue serving. (The Italians know that here the voice must be raised in mock anger in order to stave off the incoming ladle.)

The meal ends with Elsa's delicious *torta della nonna*: a lovely pastry cream in a sweetened short crust, crisscrossed on top. After this, restless children leave the dining room to run about outside while grownups linger—more or less unable to budge. A bowl of fruit and an entire wheel of *semi-stagionato* pecorino are set down on the table. Grappa last, poured into small, thick glasses: a *digestivo* that sends the guests home, finally, with smiles of deepest contentment.

the narrow via Fonte Secca, is one I visited often; there I found finely detailed silver ornaments, charms, frames, and more (I still have a few tucked away as presents for friends).

The Padrichelli *salumeria* (known formally as "Tutto Tartufo") is on the via Arco di Druso, just off the Piazza Mercato. The smell upon entering the door is unforgettable: sweet and yet goaty, salty, intense. I knew I was right at home there when Giancarlo Padrichelli, a substantial man in a small white cap and a big white apron, delicately took a piece of *ricotta salata* in his thick fingers, sprinkled crumbled *crusca* (bran) over it, and popped it into my mouth. "Try this, *signora*," he suggested, knowing full well that no one could possibly resist. I had never tasted anything like it: it was heavenly. The *salumeria*, owned by Giancarlo and his brother, is a regular stop for market-goers in Spoleto. Pungent sausages and prosciuttos hang from the ceiling, and its glass cases are filled with cheeses from every part of Umbria.

Giancarlo's son, Lorenzo, played a vital role in our travels in Umbria. A native of Spoleto, Lorenzo was working one summer at the Festival dei Due Mondi, where he met Andra Lunde, an American cellist and alumna of the New World Symphony. They married and had a baby, David, and now they live in Dayton, Ohio, where Andra is the principal cellist with the Dayton Philharmonic Orchestra. Lorenzo was the perfect liaison for our Umbrian trips: he helped us find stunning and little-known locations for both concerts and photo shoots in his home territory. The long-standing connections that he and his sister Barbara have with the region opened many doors for us. They are extremely proud of their home, and noted with pleasure as the best Umbrian wines and foods were enjoyed by their "guests." At the same time, I think that Lorenzo saw Umbria anew while working as part of the NWS team. The Castello dell'Oscano had been unknown to him ("When did they move *this* here?" he joked), and other locations—Perugia, Bevagna, Orvieto—which had once seemed distant and grand, now became familiar and human for him as working sites. It is clear that his father, Giancarlo, who long wished for his son to take over the *salumeria* someday, now grudgingly admires Lorenzo's choices.

During an outing to Perugia, I took the young musicians to meet Dr. Gianfranco Cialini at the university library. Rick Basehore completely charmed the devoted academic—who had been slightly nervous about having a group of rambunctious young Americans visit this trove of ancient volumes—by taking out his oboe and nonchalantly playing the tune from the library's treasured fourteenth-century parchment. Neil captured the visit with some wonderful photographs.

Later in the same week, the musicians gave the first concert of the 2006 Umbrian season at the university's *chiesa*: Debussy's *Syrinx* (with Ebonee Thomas on solo flute), and his Trio for Flute, Viola, and Harp; Britten's Quartet for Oboe, Violin, Viola, and Cello; and finally Ravel's Introduction and Allegro for Harp, Strings, Flute, and Clarinet. While MTT could not travel with us in the 2006 season, the musicians— consummate professionals—were nonetheless confident and on top of their game. (At the church there is a wonderful sculpture of Bepi's ancestor, Bartolo da Sassoferrato, whose formidable presence added gravitas to the occasion.)

The young travelers loved Perugia. During our days there, they explored it all, riding the escalator from the top of the Corso Vannucci down into the city's Etruscan underground.

They investigated the small shops; savored the famous beet-infused *paste caramelle rosse* at their favorite restaurant, La Taverna; and wandered the rooms of the Galleria Nazionale, where they encountered the work of hometown hero Pietro Vannucci—better known as Perugino. They sat on the broad steps by the Fontana Maggiore just beside the *duomo*, along with the rest of the young people in town. The GBang production crew—by now our fast friends—showed them the local nightclubs, and the young NWS members were amazed and delighted at the action that went on all night. They fit right in.

Among this year's group of musicians were two who found love in Umbria. Travis Gore, our tall, lanky double-bass player, met Lucia Cingolani, who was working with us as the makeup artist for Neil's shoots. During the course of the summer, they spent more and more time together. After the season was over, they married and set up house in Seattle, where Travis now plays with the Seattle Symphony Orchestra. They visit Spoleto regularly to see Lucia's family; Travis says that with each trip "it becomes more and more like a second home." And Emilia Mettenbrink, a beautiful violinist, was swept away by Fabrizio Calandri, a member of the GBang crew. I will never forget Emilia sailing breathlessly into a beauty salon off one of Spoleto's little streets, where I was having my hair blown dry. She was bubbling with happiness, in that first bloom of love—which for a musician takes a very distinct form: "I am playing Bach so much better now!" she blurted out, laughing.

The troupe performed an all-Mozart program at Spoleto's grand Teatro Caio Melisso. It occurred to me, watching them dressed in their finery onstage, that this theater had witnessed so many performances, so much music, in its 350-year history—and how truly amazing that Mozart could be present here: channeled today through the instruments and spirits of these gifted performers. It has been said that music is apart from time and place—the composer Henri Rabaud put it well: "Musical compositions . . . do not inhabit certain countries, certain museums, like paintings and statues. The Mozart Quintet is not shut up in Salzburg: I have it in my pocket." In Spoleto's Caio Melisso, too, I felt that the music was close enough to hold in my hand, and that Mozart himself was with us, breathing somewhere in the room.

101   *Leaving Him Behind* (Emilia Mettenbrink, Dustin Budish), Villa Paradiso, near Silvignano

Piano Grande, Parco Nazionale dei Monti Sibillini,
with Castelluccio in the distance

Our hearts were always heavy when we had to leave a place we had grown to love—that is, until we saw our next stop.

From our base in Spoleto we moved on to Titignano, a little-known spot that can only be described as stunning. Situated at the top of a hill between Orvieto and Todi, Titignano consists of just a handful of buildings surrounding a cobblestone courtyard: a tiny stone church, a few houses, and a magnificent medieval *castello*, which now functions as an *agriturismo*, overlooking green, cultivated valleys in every direction, with the clarion blue Lago di Corbara in the distance. The nearby farms and vineyards supply fresh vegetables, cheeses, and wine to the Agriturismo Castello di Titignano, where at meals all the guests sit together at long tables in a grand *salone* under frescoed ceilings and enjoy course after course. Alucia Scalzo remarked that it felt like one big family.

Neil's photographs from Titignano are, I think, among the most dramatic of all his Umbrian images. He reenvisioned Piero della Francesca's famous pair of portraits of Federico da Montefeltro (played by Travis Gore) and his wife, Battista Sforza (played by Julie Smith, her hair painstakingly braided and wound in Piero's style). And in Titignano's little piazza, Neil staged an elaborate Renaissance Jewish wedding, with Naomi Gray as the coy bride (in a pale coral wedding dress and headpiece) and Jerome Gordon as the groom (stately in black, looking every bit the regal prince). The nuptials were officiated by none other than Neil himself, wearing a purple headdress and robe. Jerome was skeptical about being photographed at first. "I hate to say it," he commented wryly, "but a good musician by no means makes a good model." In the end, however, he was convinced. "Looking at the photos now, Neil certainly knew what he was doing. Seeing him re-create these historic works of art, watching the wheels turn in his mind was impressive. His imagination was boundless."

That boundless imagination took us deep into the forest of Visso, where Ebonee Thomas posed as a magical Pied Piper, leading a coterie of white rabbits in a jig. Neil charmed the entire ensemble of musicians into waiting patiently for the sun to move to just the right position at the

After Leonardo's "Mona Lisa" (Emilia Mettenbrink), Patrico sul Monteluco

106 *The Pied Piper* (Ebonee Thomas), Visso

TRUFFLES

The rare *tartufo*—a star of high-end Umbrian cuisine—has magical properties that set it apart from other fungi. Shriveled, brown, frankly ugly, smelling of dank wood and earth, as small as a nut or as large as an orange (and very rarely as hefty as a small melon), the truffle has an intense and complex flavor that permeates whatever it comes near. If you are lucky enough to procure a fresh one, you may store it in an airtight jar with raw rice or whole eggs in their shells: those absorbent foods will take on the scent of the treasure, stretching both the flavor of the truffle and the pretty penny you will have spent on it.

Truffles have been sought and found in Umbria since Roman times. The local forests provide just the right conditions for them to grow: the soil is rich, and there is a proliferation of oaks, walnuts, poplar, linden, and other truffle-nourishing trees. There are at least ten different species of the jewel in Umbria, the most precious being the black *Tuber melanosporum Vittadini*.

Most Umbrian cooks agree: you must not grate or chop this truffle, only crush it—and only then can you cook it. By contrast, the white truffle, *Tuber magnatum pico*—which grows near Orvieto and Gubbio, and in the Tiber Valley—should not be crushed, but shaved, and never cooked (though it may be gently warmed in olive oil or by its closeness to hot foods).

Every February the town of Norcia celebrates truffles with its Sagra del Tartufo Nero. There, truffles are bought and sold like rare gems, and vast ongoing meals are arranged to highlight the subtleties and range of this delicacy—with truffles worked into every course, from the truffled risotto starter to an airy truffle mousse to veal with truffle sauce. One of the classic Umbrian recipes is *trota al tartufo*. Like most dishes of the region, its implementation is fairly simple and its ingredients are few—but those ingredients must be of the very finest quality, gathered and prepared with love and integrity.

Trota al Tartufo
Serves 4

Ingredients
4 whole trout, cleaned, bones in
1 cup white wine
4 tablespoons olive oil
2 cloves garlic, peeled and crushed
    or chopped fine
2 anchovy fillets
1 small black truffle, crushed to a
    rough paste with a mortar and pestle
Salt and pepper to taste

Place the fish in a large poaching pan that will hold them all without crowding. Poach in wine (if necessary, add water until the liquid reaches nearly to the tops of the fish) for 10 to 12 minutes.

Carefully remove the meat from the bones: with a sharp, flexible knife, cut a slit down the fish's spine and the meat will come loose and may be eased off the bones (the skin may be left on). Place the fillets on a serving dish.

Heat the oil with the garlic. When the garlic becomes aromatic, remove from heat and add the anchovy fillets. Agitate the anchovies to disintegrate them.

Add the truffle, freshly crushed, to the sauce. Adjust seasoning with salt and pepper (n.b. the anchovies are salty; do not oversalt). Do not reheat the sauce.

Pour sauce over the trout fillets and serve hot.

Roman Ponte d'Augusto near Narni, for a photograph that has been fondly dubbed *The Triumph of Venus*. He stirred up an evocative visual narrative of flirtation at the Villa Paradiso near Silvignano, at the end of which Emilia Mettenbrink rides off on a motorcycle, looking disdainfully back at her forlorn admirer, Dustin Budish.

One photo shoot took us up to the hill of Patrico sul Monteluco. There, Neil took advantage of the backdrop—green mountaintops facing a range of other mountaintops—to photograph Emilia as a kind of alternate Mona Lisa, with a violin under her arm (Emilia, it turned out, could evoke quite as mysterious a smile as Leonardo's model). And on the crest of the hill, Alucia was posed as a dreamy female "Peer Gynt," with a long wisp of silk flowing from her headdress. A few locals had wandered to this spot to see what we were up to. As we waited for the wind to die down so that Alucia's silk wouldn't wave about, I watched a dog digging in the dirt nearby, and his master—a grizzled old man in a dusty hat—praising him: his puppy had just found an enormous white truffle in the ground. In Umbria, I thought, what treasures spring from the very ground beneath our feet.

It was on this night that I drove to the Agriturismo Bartoli, where this narrative began. We were nearing the end of our Umbrian adventure, and I welcomed the idea of having a night to myself to think over the events of the past two years. I enjoyed a hearty supper in the *agriturismo*'s dining room, and soon after—tired, and dizzied by the Italian chatter—I bade goodnight to the Bartoli family and made my way to bed.

I slept soundly and woke to a morning of memories. When I finally opened my bedroom shutters, the pink light of dawn was reaching over the horizon, casting long and complicated shadows over the golden land. I breathed deeply, loving and relishing this place.

Our Umbrian project would wind down in the easternmost part of the region, where it touches Le Marche. For the next days, I stayed just outside the town of Norcia, at Il Casale degli Amici, run by the very kindly Ernesto Amici. The inn is set on a spectacular golden hillside and provides a small daily miracle in the form of breakfast: it includes a beautiful array of baked goods, homemade *marmellate,* and—be still my heart—freshly churned, sweet, warm ricotta cheese, which is delivered to the dining

room every morning at 7:45. (It took me no time to be trained to appear at the breakfast table very punctually, breathlessly awaiting that delivery.)

Norcia, the birthplace of St. Benedict, is known for its truffles and *salumi* products (the word *norcineria* is used throughout Italy for purveyors of the best meats). To the east of the town are the Monti Sibillini, which surround the Piano Grande, a wide-open plain. Bepi had originally suggested that Neil and I come here. He showed us photographs of an unearthly terrain: an enormous, smooth field striped with red poppies, yellow-green lentil flowers, and blue cornflowers, and edged by vast, craggy mountains. Neil and I felt it was certainly worth having a look.

The road going east from Norcia leads into the Parco Nazionale dei Monti Sibillini and twines its way uphill. After perhaps an hour of climbing, we came to the top of a mountain and before us, suddenly, was spread a massive bowl of intense green. Though it was June and very warm when Neil and I first visited, the encircling Sibilline mountains in the distance were topped with snow. Rising from the plain on its own small hill, near the center of the bowl, is the ancient village of Castelluccio. Having seen many breathtaking vistas during my Umbrian travels, I can say without hesitation that this was the most astonishing. Although we had missed the peak of colorful blossoms, the view was unforgettable exactly as it was, and we were speechless. It has been said of this place that "its beauty does not sneak up on you, but hits you with the full force of a northern blizzard"—but to me this was more like discovering a new and unimagined kind of light.

So we brought the musicians to the Piano Grande. Neil dressed them in colorful costumes like a band of traveling minstrels; a herd of sheep and a white ox were their costars. A pleasant wind moved easily across the plain. With the green fields behind them and the mountains in the distance, the musicians laughed and played their instruments, happy and relaxed. These young people's routines can be grueling, but their love of music keeps them moving forward. That love is palpable in Neil's photographs from that day.

What a glorious place from which to say good-bye.

The Visitation, La Scarzuola

After those last shots, the musicians, camera team, production crew, and I packed up and returned to our starting points.

Neil and his assistant Max went home to Israel, some of the NWS members went off to new gigs, others returned to finish their stints with the academy. And I returned to Miami to settle back in.

There had been much activity while I was gone: the ground had been broken on 17th Street in Miami Beach for the New World Symphony's new campus, designed by Frank Gehry. MTT's dream of an innovative music laboratory was coming to life. The building was conceived as a collaborative project between two lifelong friends: Gehry and MTT have known each other since Gehry babysat for Michael when they were both kids (and you can sit in on a conversation between them by playing the enclosed DVD, *Michael Tilson Thomas & Frank Gehry: A Dream Constructed*).

I had been studying the designs for the building during my travels in Italy and loved them. With his energetic and playful signature style, Gehry had brilliantly accommodated everything the NWS needs: practice spaces, gathering areas, the magnificent glowing performance hall, all wired for Internet2—twenty-first-century technology that will allow for connection with other musicians all over the world. One of my favorite aspects of the campus is the six-story-high screen on the outside of the building, on which the passing public will be able to watch what's happening onstage inside and listen to the music during concerts. A park faces the screen: here people may sit on benches and enjoy music in the open air—with no need to buy a ticket, no reserved seats. It recalls the initial vision for this Umbrian project: to seduce new ears and eyes to the world of classical music by bringing the music right to them and by removing the sense that this world is for "insiders" only.

My own way of listening has changed so much in recent years. Shortly after my return to Miami, the New World Symphony and MTT performed Tchaikovsky's Symphony no. 5 at the Adrienne Arsht Center for the Performing Arts. I sat in on one of the rehearsals, and then attended both the Saturday evening and the Sunday afternoon performances. I found myself intently studying the musicians with their instruments, listening for the sounds each was making to contribute to the whole. It was easy to feel MTT's love of this music; he was at one with it, and so were the young musicians. The symphony got under my skin as I focused on it and became familiar with it. I have listened to it many times since then, and now I anticipate the two clarinets that open the first movement, the French horn's haunting solo in the second—I have begun to make it my own. MTT often refers to the piece as "Tchaik 5"; I now feel it is a close enough acquaintance that I may call it by the same nickname.

MTT is a born teacher, and his joy in music is infectious. In the DVD *Keeping Score: MTT on Music*, he takes us behind the scenes with the San Francisco Symphony as it prepares for a performance of Tchaikovsky's Symphony no. 4 ("Tchaik 4"), leading up to the concert itself. Part of the inspiration in the film—and one reason why it is included with this volume—is MTT's extraordinarily articulate discussion of the meaning of this symphony. He effectively removes any doubt that the piece has a universal message to convey—and assures those of us who might once have felt alienated, or even (in Menotti's words) "repelled," by the world of classical music that we are not only welcome here but, as human beings, naturally part of the life that Tchaikovsky is investigating so masterfully. It is a very moving and illuminating lesson, and I encourage all of you, as soon as you have put this book down, to pop the DVD into a player.

I feel as though I have a new friend, or a new love—and, in fact, I suppose that is the case. Up to now, music has always been somewhere in the background of my life; now it is a central focus. I hunger for it. I listen closely to themes, tunes, and sounds, learning how to understand and feel the emotions that are evoked in great compositions. I have been watching films about composers and poring through a number of recent publications that shed light on how and why we listen to music— from Alex Ross's *The Rest Is Noise: Listening to the Twentieth Century* and Lawrence Kramer's *Why Classical Music Still Matters* to Oliver Sacks's *Musicophilia: Tales of Music and the Brain* and neuroscientist

Adele Diamond's studies of the effects of music on developmental cognition. Eric Jensen's fascinating *Arts with the Brain in Mind* makes the powerful point that academic curricula that emphasize music (as well as the visual and kinetic arts) have a crucial and quantifiable positive effect on behavior and learning among young people. In this era, when more and more schools, struggling with reduced budgets, have been lopping off their arts programs, we would do well to keep these results in view.

In the meantime, I could not be prouder of the NWS's efforts to get the word out to the world. The new campus, slated to open in January 2011, will usher in a fresh era for classical music, in terms of how it is learned, appreciated, disseminated, and loved. I plan to be among the first in line to experience this new way of perceiving music.

Also included with this book is a DVD titled *Music al Fresco*, which was made during the course of our 2005 Umbrian tour. I personally have watched the film many, many times, whenever I want to be instantly transported back to Umbria: to the music, the wine and food, the landscapes, and the company of a wonderfully spirited group of young musicians. Violinist Marc Rovetti—who moved on from the NWS after that Umbria trip and is now with the Philadelphia Orchestra—said something I think is very valuable about this DVD: it shows "classical musicians as down-to-earth human beings, and, most importantly, something young people can be excited about." Classical music is not dead and not out of reach; it is alive and well and ready to embrace you. This, he said, "will undoubtedly be eye-opening for many people." I believe he is right.

I am grateful to the talented and passionate artists with whom I had the privilege to travel in Umbria, and indeed to all the New World Symphony musicians, for helping to open my eyes, my ears, and my heart.

Frank Gehry's New World Symphony campus under construction, 2009.
119 (Photograph by Rui Dias-Aidos, REDAV)

120   Frank Gehry and MTT look over plans for the New World Symphony campus. (Photograph by Greg Hark)

121   Renderings of the New World Symphony campus

AFTERWORD

Neil Folberg

Who could ask for a more interesting experience? My wife, Anna, and I were invited by Lin Arison to accompany her on a trip to Umbria with Michael Tilson Thomas. To do anything with Lin is an adventure: I have never met a woman more creative, more determined to discover the essence of life in its many guises, or better prepared to enjoy and learn from every experience, positive or negative. Throw in concerts by the New World Symphony and a chance to meet the orchestra's conductor— this was going to be the trip of a lifetime.

Having collaborated with Lin on other projects, I am always prepared to go anywhere with her and be involved with any plan that she can imagine. I know that working with her will expand my horizons and vision and lead to creative challenges; in short, both my life and my work are enhanced by collaboration with Lin. With the Umbria project, it was clear from the beginning that there was no point trying to figure out in advance what to expect or to fully understand what Lin had in mind. I have learned from her just to let things happen and enjoy the process of living and discovering worlds beyond my own—worlds that will inevitably enrich me if I am open to them. So I opened myself to them. And that is probably the message of this book.

Lin has described those journeys and her aspirations fully in the preceding pages, but I can tell you what she asked of me and how I integrated her vision with mine in order to create these images. She told me that she wanted images that portrayed the youthful vitality of the musicians of the New World Symphony, the joy of music and life, set not in the confined interior of a concert hall but in the verdant, rolling landscape of Umbria, because that landscape itself is musical. At first, I thought the insistence on using the Umbrian landscape setting a little perplexing: what did these young, mostly American musicians have to do with Italy?

The connection was certainly not the musicians, but rather the *theme*, and the theme, for me, had to be visual. I looked to Italian art for inspiration and found it in the Renaissance. I had always wondered why so many portraits from this period were set in the landscape and not in an interior. It seems odd to a modern sensibility: if an artist wishes to portray an individual and say something personal about the subject, the obvious setting would seem to be the subject's own intimate, personal space. The most famous example of a Renaissance portrait set before a landscape is of course Leonardo's *Mona Lisa*. There, and in many other paintings of the period, the landscape in the background might seem an envisioned, fantasized setting—until you have visited those places in Italy. Then you see that this is the reality of the land here: those trees, those shapes, those colors. You can follow the tradition of landscape settings backward to a time before portraits of ordinary folks became common—a time when only the nobility and religious figures were immortalized through portraiture. The Holy Family was usually depicted out of doors, in a setting that represented the Holy Land (though it was usually based on the landscapes of the artist's home). The outdoor setting became a common element in portraiture that carried through into the late Renaissance.

This was the chief element that led me to Renaissance themes in these photographs, but there were others. Music played a central role for many Renaissance artists, from Fra Angelico to Caravaggio, as a symbol of something both sublime and dangerously hedonistic: a heavenly gift and an invitation to licentiousness. Food—and every other sensual

Wedding at Titignano. **Top:** *Arrival of the Bride* (Naomi Gray).
124   **Bottom:** *The Ring* (Naomi Gray, Neil Folberg, Jerome Gordon)

125   *After Piero della Francesca* (Travis Gore and Julie Smith), Titignano

pleasure—often carried a similar duality of meaning. So I had found all the elements I needed to connect our themes of youth and joy, music and landscape, spirituality and sensuality, with those of the Italian Renaissance—all set in a fantasy world of light and spirit.

After that initial trip with Lin and Michael, I was invited to Miami to meet and help select the first group of NWS musicians for our project. I began by watching rehearsals, seeing how MTT interacted with the orchestra and the individual musicians. I sat down with him, and he told me what kind of concerts he was planning in Umbria and what instruments were needed for a workable chamber ensemble. He invited my participation in selecting the musicians, and I threw myself into the task. I sat with the orchestra during rehearsals so that I could watch and hear the musicians at close range and in some sense participate in their experience. MTT asked that I keep a constant eye on what he was doing, to make sure that I never blocked his line of sight if I moved around. I sat with the orchestra for a full week of rehearsals, taking notes, absorbing the young performers' personalities, feeling the music of a full symphony orchestra throb inside my being. It was exhilarating, uplifting, and totally absorbing, like being at sea in a small ship riding the waves—and yes, I was queasy, always nervous that I was disturbing or distracting. But, although the musicians wondered what in the world I was doing there, they seemed to take my presence in stride.

At the end cf that week, I handed MTT the list of musicians I'd chosen. Aware that I know little about classical music, he asked what my criteria had been. I explained that I hadn't been looking only at people—I was seeking *passionate* performers, ones who seemed to put their entire physical being into the music. My sense was that if they could perform as musicians, they would be able to perform as actors and models. That list was honed by MTT, and the final selection fulfilled both the orchestra's musical requirements and my visual needs.

Lin and I sat down to meet with the selected group of musicians and tell them about the Umbria project. They could hardly believe what they were being offered as I described the plan to them. Lin was bemused, very much enjoying the scene and our interaction. You could see the look on her face, a sly smile that said everything. She had set up yet another creative venture, one that would challenge and excite everyone who participated in it, and she was already enjoying the process. Then I understood: she wanted me to help her create an event even more than she wanted me to make the photographs. That is remarkable. The Umbria project was now not only Lin's fantasy, but mine. It belonged also to all these beautiful young musicians who looked at me so earnestly that day in Miami.

Our time together in Umbria was unforgettable. The confluence of story, images, music, art, pageantry, and fantasy between the covers of this book conveys some of the magic that happened over the course of our two extraordinary summers in Umbria.

ACKNOWLEDGMENTS

This book is filled with the names of people and friends both in Italy and at home: my gratitude goes to all of them. I am particularly thankful to the kind Umbrians who took our party under their wings and opened their homes and their hearts to us, allowing us to enjoy a very personal journey into their culture and their breathtaking landscapes. And to all the young musicians who took part in this project, thank you for your musical gifts, and for joining in the adventure with such good spirit.

Of those who are not mentioned in these pages, I wish to thank Kirk Simon and Karen Goodman, whose filmmaking talents have provided a long-standing affirmation of our shared visions. Our collaboration on the DVD *Michael Tilson Thomas & Frank Gehry: A Dream Constructed* was a joy. I am grateful too to Michael Skor, who filmed *Music al Fresco* during our 2005 visit to Umbria (and whose footage was then edited by Emily Williams at Simon & Goodman Picture Company), and to the San Francisco Symphony staff who allowed us to include *Keeping Score: MTT on Music* with this book.

I loved traveling with Gunilla Antonini on my early exploratory visit to Umbria; she and her husband, Corrado, have been marvelous hosts in Italy, and I am indebted to Gunilla for her understanding of the terrain and her sense of adventure. The late Maria Teresa Berdondini created the itinerary for my first trip to Umbria and Tuscany when I was scouting for a travel story. That itinerary planted many of the seeds for this project. Maria Teresa's selections were always delicious; I am fortunate to have had such a knowledgeable and lively guide. Giuseppe Massa, who worked alongside Maria Teresa for years, now runs the company Charming Italy. Cheryl Alexander is another Umbria lover who kindly provided recommendations of interesting regional sites and establishments. I also thank Andrea Tana who showed me Umbria from her painterly soul. And I am grateful to Dominique Blanc, who gave me valuable advice on films to watch about the lives of composers.

Many people helped with the arrangements during our travels, which entailed not only hotels, meals, and transportation, but also rehearsals, concerts, and photo shoots. The entire team is indebted to Adam Zeichner, the New World Symphony's director of operations and personnel, who shepherded us all with wonderful good humor, and whose supreme organization was invaluable to the success of the project. Lorenzo Padrichelli played a pivotal role as both a member of the NWS family and a native Umbrian; without his collaboration, many of the region's wonders might never have been known to us. I thank Lorenzo for welcoming us all so proudly into his beautiful homeland. I am forever grateful, too, to my extraordinary assistants, Tracey Corwin in the United States and Avital Moses Shahar in Israel; I don't know where I would be without them.

I owe thanks to Allen Hoffman, editor, teacher, and friend, who traveled with Neil Folberg and me on an early trip to Italy for this project. I learned much from Allen about how to write a book, and without him, this one might never have happened.

This volume is truly a product of artistic collaboration on many levels: musical, visual, and literary. It has been such a pleasure to work again with photographer Neil Folberg, and to experience the brilliant synthesis of ideas that he brought to bear in Umbria. Neil managed to draw together music, landscape, venerable artistic traditions, sensuality, fantasy, and humor in the wonderful photographs in these pages. It is a delight to see him in action. He worked closely with Max Richardson, lighting designer extraordinaire, who provided both conceptual and technical assistance. Bénédicte Gerin was responsible for many of the production details, which were considerable on this project. I know that Neil shares my thanks to the Umbrians, the musicians, and everyone else who played a part in this project.

My co-writer, Diana Stoll, contributed an insider's understanding and genuine love of Umbria, where she has lived, worked, and explored extensively. Our travels together throughout the region in the course of developing this book were unforgettably enjoyable—how important and how good it is to work with someone who is on the same wavelength! The friendship and trust that we have formed in the process of this collaboration are icing on the cake—or, I should say, cream on the *crescionda*.

My thanks go also to Michelle Dunn Marsh, whose graceful design sensibility brings beauty, vitality, and coherence to this multifaceted volume. It has been terrific to work with her again. We are all indebted too to the Chronicle team who helped to bring the book to light.

I am most grateful to the New World Symphony and to the orchestra's fearless leader, Michael Tilson Thomas, without whom this project would have been a different and far less wonderful endeavor. It was a great privilege to spend time with Michael and Joshua Robison in Umbria, and Michael's participation in this publication, including his fascinating conversation with Frank Gehry in the enclosed DVD, has added immeasurably to the meaning and value of this project. As we look toward the opening of Gehry's beautiful New World Symphony campus and performance space in Miami Beach, my profoundest thanks and admiration go to both Michael and Frank for their enormous talents, drive, and vision.

—L.A.

While there are many people without whose help this book could not have happened, it is of course Lin Arison who gave it life, and my first and deepest thanks go to her.

From our very first meeting, over dinner in New York, this project began to shimmer with possibility. We were discussing something unrelated, when Lin looked at me rather probingly and said, "Well, you know, what I'm *really* interested in right now is Umbria." Now this was a bit uncanny, because I'd never met Lin before and she knew very little about me—certainly not, for example, that I had lived in Umbria for a long stretch with my husband and was already madly in love with the region. "Umbria!" I said . . . and so a long conversation began, and with it a friendship that has deepened over the subsequent years as this project has taken shape. I have learned in that time almost to expect the uncanny with Lin. The Italians have a beautiful word, *tempismo*, which translates somewhat prosaically to "good timing." Lin is the embodiment of *tempismo*: things just seem to fall into place when she is around—although I have stopped crediting this to mere luck and now see it as one factor of her extraordinary generosity of spirit. Lin: thank you for so much, including your understanding that many disparate passions could come together and maybe even make sense between the covers of this book.

It has been a wonderful pleasure to work again with Neil Folberg and to observe him and Max Richardson in the field as some of the photographs in this book were being created. I thank Neil and our mutual friend Stevan Baron for inviting me to work on Lin's last publication, *Travels with Van Gogh and the Impressionists*. That book's team is largely reunited for this Umbria project, including the essential component of our brilliant designer and publishing guru, Michelle Dunn Marsh, who brings sense to beauty and beauty to sense, and makes it all seem so easy as she does so. Michelle's intelligence and initiative have been indispensable to this project.

130

I am grateful to the many friends in Italy who have been so welcoming over the years, among them Siliano Stanganini, who first suggested that my husband and I take a year or so and get to know Umbria. Massimo Farina looked after us for long periods as we stayed in his house in the nonexistent *località* of "Giorgi" (try finding it on a map). He was a vital and very integral part of our Umbrian experience. Thank you also to Alessandra Toticchi, Brunella Stanganini, Piero and Marinella Barbetti, Elsa and Luigi Palmerini, and the many other Italians who invited us so kindly into their lives.

At Chronicle, Lin and I extend our thanks to Beth Weber, Mikayla Butchart, Pamela Geismar, Catherine Huchting, and Jeff Campbell for their help in guiding this publication through its editorial and production phases and into print. We are grateful to James Martin, who custom-designed the beautiful map of Umbria that opens this book. Edie Cheng and John Kieser with the San Francisco Symphony enabled us to include *MTT on Music* with this publication. At the New World Symphony, thanks go to Beth Boleyn and Craig Hall for their help in procuring materials for this volume, and most especially to Adam Zeichner, whose notes were absolutely essential in compiling and checking the book's text, and whose company was delightful during the Umbrian odyssey.

I am grateful to Tracey Corwin and Avital Moses Shahar for their amazing help moving me and my family around the globe and for keeping everything going like clockwork.

Thanks are due also to my friends at the Aperture Foundation—especially Melissa Harris and the late Michael E. Hoffman—who allowed me more than my share of sabbatical time during several Umbrian sojourns. (Thank God for fellow Italophiles!)

My respect and gratitude go to Michael Tilson Thomas for so graciously agreeing to contribute both an introduction and film time to this book, and to Joshua Robison for his patience and help along the way. Thanks also to all the brilliant New World Symphony musicians who participated in this project and who agreed to allow their words to appear in this volume. This story largely belongs to them.

Finally, I am very grateful to my beloved husband, Jeff Kinzel, and our son, Atlas (who, though born in the States, was "made in Italy"). Like Lin, they are, in all senses, the best traveling companions imaginable.

—D.C.S.

SITES AND SOURCES

New World Symphony
New Campus
1672 Drexel Avenue
Miami Beach, FL 33139

Lincoln Theater
541 Lincoln Road
Miami Beach, FL 33139
Tel: 305-673-3330; 800-597-3331
Web: www.nws.edu

National Foundation for Advancement in the Arts (and YoungArts)
777 Brickell Avenue, Suite 370
Miami, FL 33131
Tel: 305-377-1140; 800-970-ARTS
Email: info@YoungArts.org
Web: www.nfaa.org

FOOD AND WINE

Note: When calling Italy from the United States, precede all the following phone numbers with the international dialing codes 011-39.

Azienda Agraria Marfuga (olive oil)
Viale Firenze
06042 Campello sul Clitunno (PG)
Tel: 0743-521-338; 0743-270-043
Web: www.marfuga.it

Azienda Agraria Scacciadiavoli (wine)
Località Cantinone
06036 Montefalco (PG)
Tel: 0742-378-272
Email: scacciadiavoli@tin.it

La Taverna
Via delle Streghe, 8
06015 Perugia (PG)
Tel: 075-572-4128
Email: taverna9@interfree.it

La Taverna del Pescatore
Via Flaminia Vecchia
06039 Piggi di Trevi (PG)
Tel: 0742-780-920
Web: www.latavernadelpescatore.com

Le Melograne
See Le Tre Vaselle, under Hotels and Agriturismi.

Osteria del Trivio
Via del Trivio, 16
06049 Spoleto (PG)
Tel: 0743-44-349
Web: www.osteriadeltrivio.it

Padrichelli Salumeria ("Tutto Tartufo")
Via Arco di Druso, 22
06049 Spoleto (PG)
Tel: 0743-46617

Ristorante Ottavi
Via Einaudi, 41/43
06070 San Mariano-Corciano (PG)
Tel: 075-774-718

Ristorante Umbria
Via San Bonaventura
06059 Todi (PG)
Tel: 075-894-2737

Taverna del Lupo
Via Giovanni Ansidei, 21
06024 Gubbio (PG)
Tel: 075-927-4368
Web: www.mencarelligroup.com

Vinosus
Piazzo del Duomo, 15
05018 Orvieto (TR)
Tel: 0763-341-907
Email: vinosusfratini@yahoo.it

HOTELS AND AGRITURISMI

Agriturismo Bartoli
Località Patrico sul Monteluco
06049 Spoleto (PG)
Tel: 0743-220-058
Web: www.agriturismobartoli.com

Agriturismo Castello di Titignano
Località Titignano
05010 Orvieto (TR)
Tel: 0763-308-000
Web: www.titignano.com

Castello dell'Oscano
Località Oscano
06070 Perugia (PG)
Tel: 075-584371
Web: www.oscano.com

Hotel San Luca
Via Interna della Mura, 21
06049 Spoleto (PG)
Tel: 0743-223-399
Web: www.hotelsanluca.com

Il Casale degli Amici
Vocabolo Cappuccini, 157
06046 Norcia (PG)
Tel: 0743-816-811; 328-861-2385
Web: www.ilcasaledegliamici.it

Il Castagneto
Via Bologni
06061 Pozzuolo Umbro
Castiglione del Lago (PG)
Tel: 075-959-043

Le Tre Vaselle (and Le Melograne)
Via Garibaldi, 48
06089 Torgiano (PG)
Tel: 075-988-0447
Web: www.3vaselle.it

L'Orto degli Angeli
Via Dante Alighieri, 1
06031 Bevagna (PG)
Tel: 0742-360-130
Web: www.ortoangeli.com

Poggio alle Vigne
Località Montespinello
06089 Brufa (PG)
Tel: 075-982-994
Web: www.poggioallevigne.com

Relais San Clemente
Strada Passo dell'Acqua, 34
06134 Bosco (PG)
Tel: 075-591-5100
Web: www.relais.it

Villa Aureli
Via Cirenei, 70
06071 Castel del Piano Umbro (PG)
Tel: 075-514-0444; 075-573-6707
Web: www.villaureli.it

CRAFTS AND SHOPS

Brunello Cucinelli (cashmere)
Piazza Carlo Alberto dalla Chiesa, 6
06070 Solomeo (PG)
Tel: 075-529-481; 075-697-071
Web: www.brunellocucinelli.it

Giuditta Brozzetti (weaver's studio)
Via Tiberio Berardi, 5/6
06123 Perugia
Tel: 075-40236

Mariaelisa Leboroni (printmaker)
Stationery and other items available at
fine shops throughout Umbria.

Michelangeli (woodcarvings)
Piazza del Duomo, 32 (shop)
Via Gualverio Michelangeli, 3B
(studio/showroom)
05018 Orvieto (TR)
Tel: 0763-342-660
Web: www.michelangeli.it

**Rita Cammi (silverware and
ornaments)**
Via Fonte Secca, 15
06049 Spoleto (PG)
Tel: 07-085-213

**Studio Vetrate Artistiche Moretti-
Caselli (stained glass)**
Via Fatebenefratelli 2
06121 Perugia
Tel: 347-436-9676
Web: www.studiomoretticaselli.it

MUSEUMS, CHURCHES, AND OTHER SITES

Basilica di San Francesco
Piazza di San Francesco
06081 Assisi (PG)
Tel: 075-819-901

Capella della Madonna di San Brizio
Piazza del Duomo
05018 Orvieto (TR)
Tel: 0736-341-167

Castellina di Montecapanno
Località Bosco
Strada delle Selvette, 1
06134 Bosco (PG)
Tel: 075-574-1273

Galleria Nazionale dell'Umbria
Corso Vannucci, 19
06121 Perugia (PG)
Tel: 075-574-1247
Web: www.gallerianazionaleumbria.it

Isola Maggiore
Lago di Trasimeno
Ferries from Passignano, Castiglione
del Lago, and Tuoro
Tel: 075-506-781; 800-512-141
Web: www.apmperugia.it

Museo dell'Olivo e dell'Olio
Via Garibaldi, 10
06089 Torgiano (PG)
Tel: 075-988-0300
Web: www.olio.lungarotti.biz;
www.lungarotti.it

Museo del Vino
Vittorio Emanuele, 3
06089 Torgiano (PG)
Tel: 075-988-0200
Web: www.vino.lungarotti.biz;
www.lungarotti.it

**Palazzo dei Consoli and the
Eugubian Tables**
Piazza Grande
06024 Gubbio (PG)
Tel: 075-927-4298

Parco Nazionale dei Monti Sibillini
Largo Gaola Antinori, 1
62039 Visso (MC)
Tel: 0737-972-711
Email: informazione@sibillini.net
Web: www.sibillini.net

**Santa Maria della Scarzuola
and the Città Buzziana**
Località Scarzuola
05010 Montegabbione (TR)
Tel: 0763-837-436

Teatro Caio Melisso
Piazza del Duomo, 1
06049 Spoleto (PG)
Tel: 0743-222-209

Teatro Francesco Torti
Piazza Filippo Silvestri
06031 Bevagna (PG)
Tel: 0742-368-123

**Uguccione Ranieri di Sorbello
Foundation and Museum**
Piazza Piccinino, 9
06122 Perugia (PG)
Tel: 075-573-2775
Web: www.fondazioneranieri.org

FAIRS AND FESTIVALS

FEBRUARY
**Sagra del Tartufo Nero e dei Prodotti
Tipici della Valnerina**
Norcia

MARCH
Coloriamo i Cieli (biannual)
Castiglione del Lago

APRIL
Celebrazioni Dantesche
Foligno

MAY
Festa dei Ceri
Gubbio

JUNE
Mercato delle Gaite
Bevagna

JULY
Festival dei Due Mondi
Spoleto

Umbria Film Festival
Montone

Umbria Jazz
Perugia

AUGUST
Festa di Ciacciola
Pozzuolo Umbro

Sagra della Lumaca
Cantalupo di Bevagna

CONTRIBUTORS

LIN ARISON is the author of *A Love Story in Mediterranean Israel* and *Travels with Van Gogh and the Impressionists*. With her late husband, Ted Arison, and Michael Tilson Thomas, she co-founded the New World Symphony in 1987.

DIANA C. STOLL has lived and worked for extended periods in Umbria. A writer and book editor, she contributes to such publications as *Aperture* magazine, *Photography Quarterly*, and *Art Papers*.

MICHAEL TILSON THOMAS is the conductor and music director of the San Francisco Symphony and the artistic director and co-founder of the New World Symphony. In 2010 he received a National Medal of Arts, the nation's highest award for artistic achievement.

NEIL FOLBERG'S previous publications include *And I Shall Dwell Among Them*; *Celestial Nights*; and, in collaboration with Lin Arison, *Travels with Van Gogh and the Impressionists*.

ABOUT THE NEW WORLD SYMPHONY

The New World Symphony is dedicated to the artistic, professional, and personal development of outstanding young musicians. Based in Miami Beach, the fellowship program provides top graduates of music programs in the United States and abroad with the opportunity to enhance their musical education with the finest professional training.

After an intensive three-year program of performance and training, New World Symphony fellows emerge from the experience prepared for leadership positions in orchestras and ensembles around the world. Since its founding in 1987, more than six hundred alumni have established successful careers in music, at an impressive 95 percent placement rate. Each year more than one thousand musicians compete for about thirty-five available fellowships.

As a result of its unique educational environment, the New World Symphony has achieved an international reputation by creating new models for orchestral training and performance.

The New World Symphony has performed across the United States and in Argentina, Brazil, Costa Rica, France, Great Britain, Israel, Japan, Monaco, and, of course, Italy.

Library of Congress Cataloging-in-
Publication Data available.
ISBN: 9780984531615

Manufactured in Singapore.

Design by Michelle Dunn Marsh.
This book has been set in Neutraface,
designed by House Industries, Inc.

Front cover: Neil Folberg, *The Little Cellist*
(Tamar Levi), Spoleto, 2006 (detail).
Endpapers: Frank Gehry, drawing for the
New World Symphony campus.
Pages 2–3: Neil Folberg, Villa Aureli,
Castel del Piano.

10 9 8 7 6 5 4 3 2

Chronicle Books LLC
680 Second Street
San Francisco, California 94107
www.chroniclebooks.com

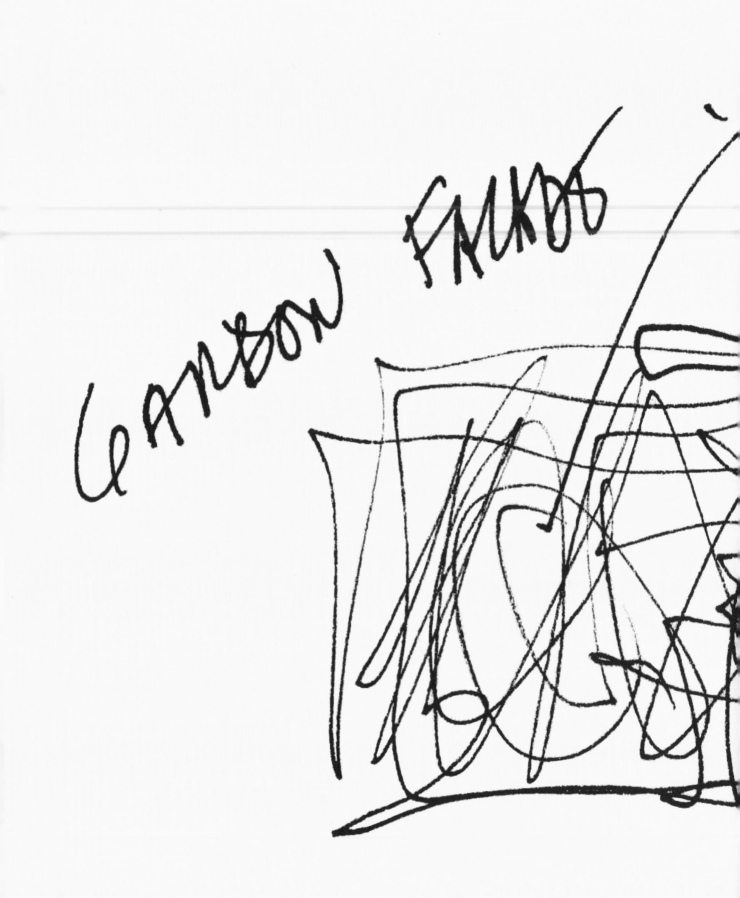